Reader's Digest
Perfect
Poultry

Reader's Digest
Perfect Poultry

Published by The Reader's Digest Association Limited
London • New York • Sydney • Montreal

Perfect Poultry is part of a series of cookery books called
Eat Well Live Well and was created by Amazon Publishing Limited.

Series Editor *Norma MacMillan*
Volume Editor *Norma MacMillan*
Art Director *Bobbie Colgate Stone*
Photographic Direction *Bobbie Colgate Stone*
Designer *Giles Powell-Smith*
Editorial Assistants *Zoe Lehmann, Anna Ward*
Nutritionists *Fiona Hunter BSc Hons (Nutri.), Dip. Dietetics,
Jane Thomas BSc, M Med Sci, SRD*

Contributors
Writers *Sara Buenfeld, Anne Gains, Beverly LeBlanc, Sara Lewis,
Sally Mansfield, Janette Marshall, Maggie Mayhew, Kate Moseley,
Marlena Spieler, Susanna Tee*
Recipe Testers *Anne Gains, Clare Lewis, Heather Owen,
Maggie Pannell, Susanna Tee*
Recipe Testing Co-ordinator *Anne Gains*
Photographer *Martin Brigdale*
Stylist *Helen Trent*
Home Economist *Bridget Sargeson*

For Reader's Digest
Series Editor *Christine Noble*
Editorial Assistant *Caroline Boucher*
Production Controllers *Kathy Brown, Jane Holyer*

Reader's Digest General books
Editorial Director *Cortina Butler*
Art Director *Nick Clark*

First Edition Copyright © 1999
The Reader's Digest Association Limited, 11 Westferry Circus,
Canary Wharf, London E14 4HE www.readersdigest.co.uk

Paperback edition 2004
Paperback Art Editor *Jane McKenna*

ISBN 0 276 42887 0

Copyright © 1999 Reader's Digest Association Far East Limited
Philippines copyright © 1999 Reader's Digest Association Far East Limited

We are committed to both the quality of our products and the service we
provide to our customers. We value your comments, so please feel free to
contact us on 08705 113366, or by via our web site www.readersdigest.co.uk
If you have any comments about the content of our books, you can contact us
at: gbeditorial@readersdigest.co.uk

Notes for the reader
• Use all metric or all imperial measures when preparing a recipe,
as the two sets of measurements are not exact equivalents.
• Recipes were tested using metric measures and conventional
(not fan-assisted) ovens. Medium eggs were used, unless
otherwise specified.
• Can sizes are approximate, as weights can vary slightly
according to the manufacturer.
• Preparation and cooking times are only intended as a guide.

The nutritional information in this book is for reference only.
The editors urge anyone with continuing medical problems or
symptoms to consult a doctor.

Contents

Eating well to live well

Eating a healthy diet can help you look good, feel great and have lots of energy. Nutrition fads come and go, but the simple keys to eating well remain the same: enjoy a variety of food – no single food contains all the vitamins, minerals, fibre and other essential components you need for health and vitality – and get the balance right by looking at the proportions of the different foods you eat. Add some regular exercise too – at least 30 minutes a day, 3 times a week – and you'll be helping yourself to live well and make the most of your true potential.

Getting it into proportion

Current guidelines are that most people in the UK should eat more starchy foods, more fruit and vegetables, and less fat, meat products and sugary foods. It is almost impossible to give exact amounts that you should eat, as every single person's requirements vary, depending on size, age and the amount of energy expended during the day. However, nutrition experts have suggested an ideal balance of the different foods that provide us with energy (calories) and the nutrients needed for health. The number of daily portions of each of the food groups will vary from person to person – for example, an active teenager might need to eat up to 14 portions of starchy carbohydrates every day, whereas a sedentary adult would only require 6 or 7 portions – but the proportions of the food groups in relation to each other should ideally stay the same.

More detailed explanations of food groups and nutritional terms can be found on pages 156–158, together with brief guidelines on amounts which can be used in conjunction with the nutritional analyses of the recipes. A simple way to get the balance right, however, is to imagine a daily 'plate' divided into the different food groups. On the imaginary 'plate', starchy carbohydrates fill at least one-third of the space, thus constituting the main part of your meals. Fruit and vegetables fill the same amount of space. The remaining third of the 'plate' is divided mainly between protein foods and dairy foods, with just a little space allowed for foods containing fat and sugar. These are the proportions to aim for.

It isn't essential to eat the ideal proportions on the 'plate' at every meal, or even every day – balancing them over a week or two is just as good. The healthiest diet for you and your family is one that is generally balanced and sustainable in the long term.

Our daily plate

Starchy carbohydrate foods: eat 6–14 portions a day

At least 50% of the calories in a healthy diet should come from carbohydrates, and most of that from starchy foods – bread, potatoes and other starchy vegetables, pasta, rice and cereals. For most people in the UK this means doubling current intake. Starchy carbohydrates are the best foods for energy. They also provide protein and essential vitamins and minerals, particularly those from the B group. Eat a variety of starchy foods, choosing wholemeal or wholegrain types whenever possible, because the fibre they contain helps to prevent constipation, bowel disease, heart disease and other health problems.
What is a portion of starchy foods?
Some examples are: 3 tbsp breakfast cereal • 2 tbsp muesli • 1 slice of bread or toast • 1 bread roll, bap or bun • 1 small pitta bread, naan bread or chapatti • 3 crackers or crispbreads • 1 medium-sized potato • 1 medium-sized plantain or small sweet potato • 2 heaped tbsp boiled rice • 2 heaped tbsp boiled pasta.

Fruit and vegetables: eat at least 5 portions a day

Nutrition experts are unanimous that we would all benefit from eating more fruit and vegetables each day – a total of at least 400 g (14 oz) of fruit and vegetables (edible part) is the target. Fruit and vegetables provide vitamin C for immunity and healing, and other 'antioxidant' vitamins and minerals for protection against cardiovascular disease and cancer. They also offer several 'phytochemicals' that help protect against cancer, and B vitamins, especially folate, which is important for women planning a pregnancy, to prevent birth defects. All of these, plus other nutrients, work together to boost well-being.

Antioxidant nutrients (e.g. vitamins C and beta-carotene, which are mainly derived from fruit and vegetables) and vitamin E help to prevent harmful free radicals in the body initiating or accelerating cancer, heart disease, cataracts, arthritis, general ageing, sun damage to skin, and damage to sperm. Free radicals occur naturally as a by-product of normal cell function, but are also caused by pollutants such as tobacco smoke and over-exposure to sunlight.
What is a portion of fruit or vegetables?
Some examples are: 1 medium-sized portion of vegetables or salad • 1 medium-sized piece of fresh fruit • 6 tbsp (about 140 g/5 oz) stewed or canned fruit • 1 small glass (100 ml/3½ fl oz) fruit juice.

Dairy foods: eat 2–3 portions a day

Dairy foods, such as milk, cheese, yogurt and fromage frais, are the best source of calcium for strong bones and teeth, and important for the nervous system. They also provide some protein for growth and repair, vitamin B_{12}, and vitamin A for healthy eyes. They are particularly valuable foods for young children, who need full-fat versions at least up to age 2. Dairy foods are also especially important for adolescent girls to prevent the development of osteoporosis later in life, and for women throughout life generally.

To limit fat intake, wherever possible adults should choose lower-fat dairy foods, such as semi-skimmed milk and low-fat yogurt.
What is a portion of dairy foods?
Some examples are: 1 medium-sized glass (200 ml/7 fl oz) milk • 1 matchbox-sized piece (40 g/1½ oz) Cheddar cheese • 1 small pot of yogurt • 125 g (4½ oz) cottage cheese or fromage frais.

Protein foods: eat 2–4 portions a day

Lean meat, fish, eggs and vegetarian alternatives provide protein for growth and cell repair, as well as iron to prevent anaemia. Meat also provides B vitamins for healthy nerves and digestion, especially vitamin B_{12}, and zinc for growth and healthy bones and skin. Only moderate amounts of these protein-rich foods are required. An adult woman needs about 45 g of protein a day and an adult man 55 g, which constitutes about 11% of a day's calories. This is less than the current average intake. For optimum health, we need to eat some protein every day.

What is a portion of protein-rich food?

Some examples are: 3 medium-sized slices (50–70 g/scant 2–3 oz) beef, pork, ham, lamb, liver, kidney, chicken or oily fish • 115–140 g (4–5 oz) white fish (not fried in batter) • 3 fish fingers • 2 eggs (up to 4 a week) • 5 tbsp (200 g/7 oz) baked beans or other pulses or lentils • 2 tbsp (60 g/2¼ oz) nuts, peanut butter or other nut products.

Foods containing fat: 1–5 portions a day

Unlike fruit, vegetables and starchy carbohydrates, which can be eaten in abundance, fatty foods should not exceed 33% of the day's calories in a balanced diet, and only 10% of this should be from saturated fat. This quantity of fat may seem a lot, but it isn't – fat contains more than twice as many calories per gram as either carbohydrate or protein.

Overconsumption of fat is a major cause of weight and health problems. A healthy diet must contain a certain amount of fat to provide fat-soluble vitamins and essential fatty acids, needed for the development and function of the brain, eyes and nervous system, but we only need a small amount each day – just 25 g is required, which is much less than we consume in our Western diet. The current recommendations from the Department of Health are a maximum of 71 g fat (of this, 21.5 g saturated) for women each day and 93.5 g fat (28.5 g saturated) for men. The best sources of the essential fatty acids are natural fish oils and pure vegetable oils.

What is a portion of fatty foods?

Some examples are: 1 tsp butter or margarine • 2 tsp low-fat spread • 1 tsp cooking oil • 1 tbsp mayonnaise or vinaigrette (salad dressing) • 1 tbsp cream • 1 individual packet of crisps.

Foods containing sugar: 0–2 portions a day

Although many foods naturally contain sugars (e.g. fruit contains fructose, milk lactose), health experts recommend that we limit 'added' sugars. Added sugars, such as table sugar, provide only calories – they contain no vitamins, minerals or fibre to contribute to health, and it is not necessary to eat them at all. But, as the old adage goes, 'a little of what you fancy does you good' and sugar is no exception. Denial of foods, or using them as rewards or punishment, is not a healthy attitude to eating, and can lead to cravings, binges and yo-yo dieting. Sweet foods are a pleasurable part of a well-balanced diet, but added sugars should account for no more than 11% of the total daily carbohydrate intake.

In assessing how much sugar you consume, don't forget that it is a major ingredient of many processed and ready-prepared foods.

What is a portion of sugary foods?

Some examples are: 3 tsp sugar • 1 heaped tsp jam or honey • 2 biscuits • half a slice of cake • 1 doughnut • 1 Danish pastry • 1 small bar of chocolate • 1 small tube or bag of sweets.

Too salty

Salt (sodium chloride) is essential for a variety of body functions, but we tend to eat too much through consumption of salty processed foods, 'fast' foods and ready-prepared foods, and by adding salt in cooking and at the table. The end result can be rising blood pressure as we get older, which puts us at higher risk of heart disease and stroke. Eating more vegetables and fruit increases potassium intake, which can help to counteract the damaging effects of salt.

Alcohol in a healthy diet

In recent research, moderate drinking of alcohol has been linked with a reduced risk of heart disease and stroke among men and women over 45. However, because of other risks associated with alcohol, particularly in excess quantities, no doctor would recommend taking up drinking if you are teetotal. The healthiest pattern of drinking is to enjoy small amounts of alcohol with food, to have alcohol-free days and always to avoid getting drunk. A well-balanced diet is vital because nutrients from food (vitamins and minerals) are needed to detoxify the alcohol.

Water – the best choice

Drinking plenty of non-alcoholic liquid each day is an often overlooked part of a well-balanced diet. A minimum of 8 glasses (which is about 2 litres/3½ pints) is the ideal. If possible, these should not all be tea or coffee, as these are stimulants and diuretics, which cause the body to lose liquids, taking with them water-soluble vitamins. Water is the best choice. Other good choices are fruit or herb teas or tisanes, fruit juices – diluted with water, if preferred – or semi-skimmed milk (full-fat milk for very young children). Fizzy sugary or acidic drinks such as cola are more likely to damage tooth enamel than other drinks.

As a guide to the vitamin and mineral content of foods and recipes in the book, we have used the following terms and symbols, based on the percentage of the daily RNI provided by one serving for the average adult man or woman aged 19–49 years (see also pages 156–158):

✓✓✓   or excellent   at least 50% (half)

✓✓   or good   25–50% (one-quarter to one-half)

✓   or useful   10–25% (one-tenth to one-quarter)

Note that recipes contribute other nutrients, but the analyses only include those that provide at least 10% RNI per portion. Vitamins and minerals where deficiencies are rare are not included.

Versatile Poultry

A great source of lean protein

It is no wonder that poultry today is so popular all over the world. It offers first-class protein, it provides many essential vitamins and minerals, and it is low in saturated fat – an unbeatable healthy profile. And the wonderful variety of poultry available – from well-loved chicken and turkey to duck, goose, guinea fowl, pigeon and quail – as well as game birds, such as pheasant, partridge and grouse, can be prepared in so many ways. Here, you'll find buying tips and guidelines on the preparation, storage and cooking of poultry and game birds. There are also ideas for flavourings and lower-fat preparations, and basic recipes for stock and stuffings.

Poultry in a healthy diet

Protein is essential for good health and well-being – every cell in the body needs it. Protein builds us up and keeps us strong, growing, repairing and maintaining everything from muscles and bones to skin, hair and fingernails. It does many jobs that carbohydrates and fat just cannot do. It is a vital nutrient.

Essential for life

Protein is made up of amino acids, which are compounds containing the 4 elements that are necessary for life: carbon, hydrogen, oxygen and nitrogen. We need all of the 20 amino acids commonly found in plant and animal proteins. The human body can only make 12, so the remaining 8 have to be obtained from the food we eat. The proportions of amino acids in animal foods (meat, poultry, game and game birds, fish, milk, cheese and eggs) match human requirements more closely than the amino acids in vegetable foods, even though some vegetable foods, such as nuts and pulses, are very high in protein.

Protein foods should feature daily in the diet because amino acids cannot be stored in the body for later use. Any excess is used at the time as energy or stored as body fat.

Quality, not quantity

Despite protein foods being so vital, we do not need to eat them in great quantity – no more than 15% of our daily calorie intake should be from protein. The amount allocated to protein on the daily 'plate' in a well-balanced diet is, therefore, considerably smaller than accompanying starchy carbohydrate foods (such as pasta or rice), vegetables and fruit, which for some people may mean reducing the quantity of protein foods they eat.

In the UK, the average consumption of red meat – beef, lamb, pork and veal – is 8–10 portions a week, or 85 g (3 oz) a day. Current healthy eating guidelines suggest that this is sufficient, and that the rest of the protein requirement should come from other sources, such as poultry and game, fish, eggs, dairy foods, nuts and seeds, pulses and cereals.

Just 2 portions of protein food per day is thought adequate for most people, although the very active might need 3 or 4. With only a small quantity required, it is well worth choosing the best quality protein foods to eat. Lean poultry and game birds are far better nutritional value for money than high-fat products such as savoury pies, pâté, sausages and fatty meats, and can be low-fat alternatives to other protein foods such as red meat, eggs and full-fat cheeses.

Cutting the fat

Poultry and game birds are lower in saturated fat than most red meat – most of the fat they contain is unsaturated or

▲ Removing the skin from chicken reduces the fat content considerably, even if this is done after cooking – the fat in chicken skin does not transfer to the meat during cooking

▲ In a well-balanced meal, protein foods make up the smallest portion. Here a tender duck breast with a redcurrant sauce is served with plenty of potatoes (starchy carbohydrate) and a selection of vitamin-rich vegetables

monounsaturated. Chicken and turkey are particularly lean birds, and most of their fat is in the skin, so if the visible fat and skin are removed, either before or after cooking, they are a good low-fat choice. Note, though, that if you eat both the meat and the skin of chicken and turkey, the fat content will be higher than an equivalent amount of beef or other red meat.

Duck, which is a fatty bird, can be enjoyed in a healthy diet too, if the skin and fat are removed before cooking. Once this is done, lean duck has about the same amount of fat as lamb.

Vitamins and minerals too

Poultry and game birds are an important source of B vitamins, including B_1 (thiamin), B_2 (riboflavin), niacin, B_6 and B_{12} – all essential for the body to run smoothly. They also provide many essential minerals such as zinc, iron, chromium, copper, selenium, phosphorus, potassium and magnesium. Eating lean poultry and game birds is one of the easiest ways to ensure you get enough iron, zinc and vitamin B_{12}. Chicken and turkey livers offer a lot of vitamin A too.

Popular poultry

Chicken and turkey are wonderfully versatile, and offer lean protein plus essential vitamins and minerals, as do pigeon, quail and guinea fowl. Duck and goose, with their rich dark meat, are also first-class sources of protein, and despite being fattier than other poultry, they too can be enjoyed in a healthy diet.

An ABC of poultry

Although to most people, the term poultry generally means just chicken and turkey, poultry is, in fact, the term for all domesticated birds reared for the table – even those that were wild until quite recently. Poultry, then, includes chicken, duck, goose, guinea fowl, quail, squab pigeon and turkey.

Chicken

Chicken – probably the world's most popular meat – is eaten in every country, and the range of preparations reflects this, using ingredients and flavours from all points of the globe. Today the choice of chicken to buy is wide – from fresh-chilled, intensively reared birds to organic chickens, free-range chickens and corn-fed chickens, as well as poulet de Bresse and other well-flavoured chickens from France.

Nutritionally, chicken is a very good source of protein: a 140 g (5 oz) portion of grilled breast (without skin) provides 88% RNI of protein for women and 71% RNI for men. Cooking chicken without too much additional fat and removing the skin, either before or after cooking, offers the lowest-fat option. Compare about 2 g of fat per 100 g (3½ oz) in a grilled skinless boneless chicken breast (2% fat), with 12 g of fat per 100 g (3½ oz) in a grilled chicken breast with skin (12% fat).

Although red meat is usually thought of as one of the best protein sources of vitamins and minerals, chicken compares very favourably. It is an excellent source of the B vitamin niacin: a 140 g (5 oz) portion provides more than the daily requirement for adults. It is also a useful source of vitamins B_2, B_6 and B_{12}, and the mineral zinc.

Corn-fed chickens are fed some corn (maize), but their attractive yellow-coloured flesh and fat is the result of an artificial dye in the food. A corn-fed chicken has very similar protein and fat levels to an ordinary chicken, and similar amounts of iron, zinc and B vitamins.

Chicken livers are a rich source of iron, zinc, vitamin A and many of the B vitamins, especially B_{12}. The iron present in liver is in a form that is easily absorbed by the body.

Whole chickens are best for roasting, and can also be poached, braised and pot-roasted. Young roasters are the most widely available, and one weighing 1.35–1.8 kg (3–4 lb) will serve 4–6 people.

Poussins are small, immature chickens. They are slightly lower in protein than older birds, and a little higher in fat. They do not have a lot of flavour, so need to be marinated and basted if being grilled or barbecued. Alternatively, cook them with flavourful ingredients. Allow one poussin per person.

Spring chickens, also called poulets, are a little older than poussins and thus a little bigger. One bird will feed 2 people.

Boilers, or boiling fowl, are old laying hens. Because of their age they are tougher than younger chickens, but they have much more flavour, and make delicious stock for soup. Unfortunately they are now hard to find.

Capons are neutered male birds, with a greater proportion of white meat to dark meat. Their meat is succulent as it is quite high in fat. Capons are available only from specialist outlets.

Joints are available on and off the bone, with skin or skinless. Common chicken joints are breasts (skinless boneless breasts are often called fillets), thighs, drumsticks, quarters and wings. Thigh and drumstick together are sometimes called a Maryland, and boneless breast and wing together a supreme. Breast is the tenderest meat with the least fat; thigh is the fattiest and thus most moist.

whole chicken

chicken joints   minced chicken

chicken sausages   duck joints

whole duck

Minced chicken can be used to make burgers, meat loaves, shepherd's pie and most other dishes that would traditionally use minced beef or other red meat.

Chicken products such as sausages can offer a lower-fat alternative to red meat products. They may not be as nutritious as chicken generally, however, because the meat will have been 'stretched' with bulking ingredients.

Duck

Duck has a similar protein content to chicken and turkey, but is higher in fat: roast meat contains 10% fat, even though no fat is visible, and duck meat, fat and skin together contain 29% fat. Most of the fat on a duck is found just below the skin. Although much of this fat is monounsaturated, from a health point of view it is still preferable to remove the skin and visible fat before cooking or, if roasting, to prick the skin all over before cooking to allow the fat to drain away.

Duck is rich in minerals, being an excellent source of zinc and a good source of iron, offering three times as much iron as chicken. It is also a very good source of B vitamins, and contains selenium and potassium.

The ducks we buy in butchers and supermarkets are bred for the table in sheds, in conditions almost identical to those for intensively reared chickens. They are very rarely kept free-range on ponds. The most common breed of duck in Britain is the Aylesbury. It is also possible to find Gressingham ducks (a cross between the domestic duck and the mallard) and two French breeds, the Barbary and Nantais.

Duckling was once the term for birds up to 2 months old, but it is now used until they reach 6 months. Although a duckling might be thought to have tenderer meat than a duck, this is not always the case, and being young it may not have a lot of meat on its bones. Ducklings can weigh as much as 3.2 kg (7 lb), according to the breed, although 1.5–2 kg (3 lb 3 oz–4½ lb) is more usual.

Ducks (like ducklings) do not have a lot of meat for their size, and the amount can vary according to the breed – for example, the Aylesbury is more fleshy than others. As a general guide, when buying allow about 750 g (1 lb 10 oz) per person.

Joints of duck widely available are legs and boneless breasts. The meat on duck legs is tough, so they are best used in soups and stews. The breasts can be pan-fried, grilled or barbecued – each breast will serve one – or cut up for stir-fries. The plump, meaty breasts (called magrets) from the French Moulard, the duck reared for foie gras, will each serve 2 people.

Goose

Being a waterfowl (like duck), the rich dark meat of a goose is a lot fattier than chicken and turkey. However, unlike duck, a greater proportion of goose fat is saturated, so it is particularly important to prick the skin before roasting so that the fat can run out, or to remove any visible fat and skin if cooking by other methods.

Goose has a similar protein content to other poultry. It provides as much zinc as duck and more iron – a 100 g (3½ oz) portion offers 31% RNI of iron for women and more than 50% for men. As for vitamins, goose is an excellent source of the B vitamins B_1, B_2, B_6, B_{12} and niacin.

Goslings are 6–8 months old. Being so young, they have very tender meat that is less fatty than that of older birds. Goslings weigh up to about 2.25 kg (5 lb).

Goose, in its youthful prime, will weigh 3.2–5.4 kg (7–12 lb). As the bird gets older and larger, the meat becomes tougher and more fatty. There is a lot less meat on a goose than on a chicken or turkey, so allow about 750 g (1 lb 10 oz) per person when calculating the size of bird to buy.

Guinea fowl

Semi-domesticated breeds of guinea fowl are not as lean as wild guinea fowl, which does not have a closed hunting season, but both are low in fat, particularly saturated fat. The meat of guinea fowl is like that of a slightly gamey chicken – darker than that of chicken, and with more leg meat and less breast meat. Guinea fowl is a good source of protein, and provides B vitamins and iron.

Pigeon

Pigeon, whether squab – the farmed bird – or the wild wood pigeon, is available all year, but is best between May and September. Despite being a small bird, pigeon is quite meaty, with very well-flavoured flesh. Like other poultry, it is a first-class source of protein and has a moderate fat content. Pigeon is an excellent source of iron, with a portion providing 100% RNI for both men and women, and a useful source of zinc.

Quail

Like guinea fowl and pigeon, quail is a game bird that is today bred for the table. It is very small, with delicately flavoured meat, and 2 birds are often served per person. The nutritional profile is similar to pheasant or partridge.

Turkey

While chicken has long been an everyday meat, turkey is traditionally reserved for special occasions such as Christmas and Thanksgiving. A large turkey, roasted to perfection, is the ideal bird for a festive dish – it can feed a large gathering and still leave plenty of meat for sandwiches and other meals. Smaller turkeys and turkey joints are now widely available and are well worth enjoying throughout the year.

turkey breast steaks   quail   pigeon   guinea fowl   chicken

Sizing up turkey

Judging how big a turkey to buy depends on how many people you want to serve – and the leftovers you want to enjoy over the following few days. Here is a rough guide:

2.25–3.2 kg (5–7 lb)	bird serves	6–9
3.6–4 kg (8–9 lb)	bird serves	10–11
4.5–5 kg (10–11 lb)	bird serves	12–14
5.4–6 kg (12–13 lb)	bird serves	16–18
6.2–7.6 kg (14–17 lb)	bird serves	20–24
8–9 kg (18–20 lb)	bird serves	26–30

Nutritionally, turkey is very similar to chicken, although it contains slightly more vitamin B_{12} and niacin and more zinc. The dark leg meat offers three times as much zinc as the light breast meat and twice as much iron.

There are free-range and organic turkeys available, but most are reared under intensive conditions. On a much smaller scale, some schemes exist to produce 'traditional' turkeys, which are special breeds, such as the Norfolk Black and the Cambridge Bronze. These turkeys are hung to develop flavour, and do not have water added during processing.

Whole turkeys range in size from young birds at 2.25–3.6 kg (5–8 lb) up to huge birds weighing 11.25–13.5 kg (25–30 lb). See the chart, left, for judging the size of turkey to buy.

Joints on the bone are drumsticks, thighs and breasts. They can be quite large, and one joint will probably serve 2 people. There are also boneless breast steaks, escalopes and fillets for single servings. The whole breast on the bone, without the legs and wings, is often called a crown roast.

Minced turkey makes a lower-fat alternative to red meat minces for burgers and in meat sauces for dishes such as lasagne.

Turkey products such as sausages can be a good lower-fat choice, although many are breaded and deep-fried, which makes them high in fat. Turkey 'rolls' and 'roasts' can contain a lot of additives as well as water, so check the labels.

A buyer's guide to poultry

When choosing poultry, look for fresh, unblemished skin and meat. Avoid birds with dry or discoloured skin, or skin with bruises or tears, and especially birds that have an 'off' odour. Be sure that the wrapping on pre-packaged birds isn't torn and that the package isn't leaking. If the bird is frozen, check carefully that there is no freezer burn (brown or greyish-white patches on the skin).

duck   goose   turkey

Glorious game

Britain has a wealth of native game birds, and their popularity has grown steadily along with an increasing appreciation of their healthy lower-fat attributes. Wider availability means that now you can even pick up a pheasant at your supermarket rather than having to seek out a specialist game supplier.

An ABC of game birds

Some game birds that once lived in the wild, such as quail and guinea fowl, are now reared for the table and, as such, are classed as poultry. Pheasant and partridge are often intensively reared, and then released into the 'wild' for the shooting season. Other birds remain truly wild, feeding on their traditional forage rather than on processed feed, with all the physical activity that entails. As a result, the meat of wild game birds tastes quite different from that of their farmed or 'semi-wild' counterparts, and it is more lean. It is also free of growth hormones and antibiotics.

Small young game birds – whether farmed or wild – are best roasted, or they can be grilled or barbecued. Older birds, particularly wild ones, can be tough and their meat tends to be dry, so they benefit from marinating before cooking, or a moist method of cooking such as braising or pot-roasting. Alternatively, use them in pies, soups and so on.

Hanging poultry and game birds

In the past, most meat and poultry – even fish – was 'hung', to allow the enzymes and spoilage bacteria that are naturally present to break down and tenderise the muscle, in the process contributing distinctive flavour changes. Modern methods of farming produce poultry and game birds that do not need to be hung, probably because the muscles are not as 'tough' as they are in wild birds or in some free-range produce. Traditional poulterers and game dealers still hang pheasant and wild duck, and organic and specialist chicken and turkey producers often hang poultry before it is 'dressed' (i.e. plucked and gutted).

Duck

The wild members of the duck family are much tougher and lower in fat than the duck bred for the table, but like supermarket duck the meat has a very rich flavour. Mallard is the most common and largest wild duck – one bird will serve 2–3 people. Widgeon, thought to be superior in flavour to mallard, will serve 2 at a stretch. Teal, the smallest wild duck, will serve one. The season is 1 September to 31 January.

Grouse

This small, ground-scratching game bird is hunted on moors in northern England and Scotland – the 'Glorious Twelfth' (12 August) marks the start of the shooting season, which ends on 10 December. The birds feed on heather shoots, berries and small insects, and their dark red meat is richly gamey in flavour. A young grouse weighs about 750 g (1 lb 10 oz) and will serve one person.

Grouse contains marginally more protein than poultry, and is extremely low in fat – only 5 g per 100 g (3½ oz) – most of which is unsaturated. It is an excellent source of B vitamins, with a typical 140 g (5 oz) portion providing all an adult's daily B_2 and niacin needs, as well as over half the B_1 requirements. When roasted, grouse is an excellent source of iron and a good source of zinc.

Partridge

A small game bird, the same size as grouse, partridge is perhaps best known for its appearance in a pear tree in the traditional Christmas song. In fact, Christmas is in the middle of the shooting season for partridge, which is from 1 September to 1 February. Partridge has pale meat with a delicate flavour – it is usually hung for 3–4 days before being plucked and gutted. A bird will make one serving.

Partridge has one of the highest meat protein contents, equalled only by venison, and a fat content of 7% in its meat. It is also an excellent source of both iron and phosphorus.

Pheasant

Slightly larger than most other game birds, pheasant is quite tame, and as a result is now intensively reared. The shooting season lasts from 1 October to 1 February. The meat of a pheasant has quite a gamey flavour, and modern tastes prefer unhung birds, although older birds benefit from being hung for several days to tenderise them before cooking. A pheasant weighing about 1.5 kg (3 lb 3 oz) will serve 2–3 people.

Pheasant is an excellent source of protein. It is relatively high in fat for a game bird, at 10–12%, although this is mainly monounsaturated. Generally, the plump hen (female) birds contain more fat than the cocks (males). Pheasant is lower in iron than some other game birds, but is still an excellent source, as it is for B vitamins.

Other game birds

Black game, related to grouse and similar in flavour, is about the size of a pheasant. It is native to the hills and moors of Scotland and northern England. The shooting season is 20 August to 10 December. Other game birds similar to grouse include capercailzie, or capercaillie, a large bird which is in season 1 October to 31 January, and ptarmigan, in season 12 August to 10 December.

Two of the smallest game birds are snipe (12 August to 31 January) and woodcock (1 October to 31 January). Traditionally these birds are not gutted before cooking.

Free-range vs intensive farming

Free-range poultry, in theory, contains less saturated fat and more unsaturated fat than intensively reared birds that are unable to exercise. Physical activity alters the fat profile of a bird or animal in a way that is beneficial both for its own health and for the people who eat it. However, some of the older/rarer breeds favoured by organic and free-range poultry producers are less lean than breeds used in intensive farming. Also, some systems are more free-range than others.

Chickens were originally jungle fowl, and they are not always happy roaming in a field under the open sky, which is often the only type of 'range' available, so many free-range birds in fact remain quite sedentary. In contrast, some free-range farms offer wooded areas in which the chickens are happy to roam and forage for worms and insects to supplement their feed.

Because free-range birds are less intensively fed and are slaughtered when they are older, they tend to have a better flavour than intensively reared birds.

Is organic poultry any healthier?

While all poultry and meat are monitored and controlled by government regulatory bodies (in the same way that fruit and vegetables are monitored for pesticide and other agrochemical residues), there are concerns that antibiotic residues, in particular in intensively farmed meat and poultry, may transfer drug resistance problems to humans. Organic poultry is not given antibiotics and other routine veterinary drugs, nor artificial growth-promoting hormones in its feed, and so should be free from drug residues.

partridge   grouse   pheasant   wild duck (mallard)

Handle with care

Poultry and game birds need careful handling, to be sure they are stored and prepared safely, and then cooked thoroughly. If you follow a few simple rules, you can eliminate any risk of harmful bacteria causing food poisoning, and just enjoy the nutritional and culinary benefits of these versatile, lean-protein birds.

Safe handling

Food poisoning comes from eating food contaminated with large numbers of bacteria or the toxins that some of them produce. Bacteria are naturally present in the air, water and soil and on our bodies. Because of modern intensive farming techniques, they are also widespread in meat, and particularly in poultry. The most common bacteria found in poultry are salmonella and campylobacter. Food poisoning can be caused by eating undercooked poultry or by eating lightly cooked food or raw food such as salad that has been in contact with raw poultry or its juices.

All poultry is extremely perishable, and bacteria multiply rapidly in warm conditions, so the first golden rule after buying your bird is to get it home and into the fridge as soon as possible. On a warm day, put the bird into an insulated container for the journey.

▲ Store poultry in the fridge, loosely covered so air can circulate

Storing in the fridge

If you are going to cook the bird within a few hours, you can put it into the fridge in its original wrapping. Otherwise, unwrap the bird (take any giblets out of the body cavity), put it on a plate and cover lightly with greaseproof paper or foil, or put it into a loosely covered container. Then put it into the fridge, ideally at the bottom – it is important that juices from poultry do not drip onto other food, particularly if that food will not be cooked before eating. Don't overcrowd the fridge – make sure there is room for cold air to circulate; the temperature inside should be no higher than 5°C (41°F).

In general, poultry must be cooked within 2 days of purchase – stick to the use-by date on the package, or ask your supplier for guidance.

Freezing and thawing

Poultry can be stored for up to 6 months in a freezer. Before cooking, a frozen bird must be thoroughly thawed – if it is still partially frozen, its centre will not reach a high enough temperature during cooking to destroy any food poisoning bacteria that might be present (salmonella survives freezing). Thawing should be done slowly – rapid thawing will spoil the texture of the meat, and warm conditions will encourage the growth of any bacteria.

The best way to thaw poultry is in the fridge: set the bird, still in its freezer wrapping, in a deep dish and put it in the fridge. Leave it until the wrapping is loose, then remove this and pour off any liquid that has collected in the dish. Cover the bird loosely with greaseproof paper and put it back in the fridge to continue thawing slowly. Remove any giblets as soon as they are loose, and thaw them in a separate, covered basin. Once the bird is completely thawed, it should be cooked very soon afterwards.

A guide to thawing times in the fridge

Frozen weight range	Thawing time
1.35–2.25 kg (3–5 lb)	20 hours
2.7–3.2 kg (6–7 lb)	30 hours
3.6–4 kg (8–9 lb)	36 hours
4.5–5 kg (10–11 lb)	45 hours
5.4–9 kg (12–20 lb)	60 hours

An alternative, slightly faster method of thawing is in cold water: immerse the bird in a large basin or sink of cold water (not warm), and change the water every 30 minutes or so as the bird thaws to keep it cold.

Keeping tools clean

Use a separate chopping board for raw poultry, meat and fish. This prevents bacteria that might be present in the raw food from transferring to cooked food or to other foods that are to be eaten raw. If you have to use the same board (or work surface), wash it well with hot soapy water or use an antibacterial spray between uses.

Before you start

Wash your hands thoroughly with hot soapy water both before and after handling raw poultry, and between handling raw and cooked poultry. (It is also essential to wash your hands after visiting the bathroom, after coughing, blowing your nose, or touching your face or hair, or after using cleaning products.)

A final rinse?

Current advice is that raw poultry should not be rinsed before cooking as this is thought to encourage the spread of any bacteria that might be present. If your bird seems too moist, wipe it over, inside and out, with kitchen paper.

Safe cooking

To be sure any food poisoning bacteria that might be present is killed, poultry such as chicken and turkey must be cooked thoroughly. It must never be cooked partially – if there is bacteria in the uncooked portions, it will flourish.

Stuffing

Although it was once common to stuff the body cavity of poultry – particularly turkey – before roasting, this is now not recommended, because the stuffing can prevent heat penetrating to the centre of the bird. Also, the stuffing itself can harbour bacteria, which will not be destroyed unless the stuffing reaches a safe temperature inside the bird. If you do want to stuff the cavity, fill it only two-thirds full, and weigh the bird again after stuffing to calculate cooking time. Then, after cooking, test the temperature of the stuffing with an instant-read thermometer; it should be at least 75°C (170°F). Alternatively, stuff the neck end only, or cook the stuffing separately. Do not stuff a bird more than 3 hours before cooking. If the stuffing is warm, cook the bird straightaway.

Trussing

Just tucking the wing tips under the bird's back and tying the ends of the legs loosely together is sufficient – a tight trussing may keep the bird in a neat compact shape, but it can also prevent the leg meat from cooking through as rapidly as the drier breast meat.

▲ After stuffing the neck end, secure the flap of skin in place with the wing tips rather than trussing the bird

Testing for doneness

The traditional way of testing poultry and game birds to see if they are cooked is to pierce the thickest part of the meat with a skewer or the point of a sharp knife, and then to note the colour of the juices that run out. An alternative method for a roasted bird is to lift it up with a two-pronged fork and tip it so that the juices run out of the cavity. For chicken, turkey and goose, the juices should be completely clear and not at all pink; however, for duck and many game birds served rare, the juices that run out will still be pink.

Another, more precise way to check if poultry is thoroughly cooked is to use an instant-read thermometer. At the end of the recommended cooking time, insert the thermometer probe into the thickest part of the meat. For chicken and turkey, the internal temperature of the dark thigh meat should be at least 75°C (170°F); the white meat of the breast should have reached 71°C (160°F).

▲ To freeze cooked poultry, take the meat off the bone, then pack in a rigid container, with gravy to cover completely

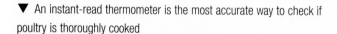

▼ An instant-read thermometer is the most accurate way to check if poultry is thoroughly cooked

If not eating immediately

As soon as chicken and turkey are cooked, they should be served and not kept warm. For leftovers, cool them as quickly as possible (2 hours maximum at room temperature). When cold, remove any stuffing, wrap the bird in foil and store in the fridge. It can be kept for 3–5 days.

Reheat cooked poultry only once. To reheat in gravy or a sauce, bring to the boil and cook for 5 minutes. Or reheat in the microwave, stirring during cooking to avoid cold spots and to ensure that the food is piping hot throughout.

For longer storage, remove the meat from the bones, put it in a freezer bag and label, then freeze. The meat can also be frozen in gravy: pack the meat in a rigid container and pour over the gravy to immerse the meat completely, then cover, leaving 2.5 cm (1 in) headroom for expansion of the frozen gravy. Or freeze in a freezer bag inside a casserole or dish, and remove the bag when frozen. Cook from frozen, thawing gently and then reheating as above.

A world of flavours

Poultry and game birds are wonderfully versatile, being suitable for many preparations and complemented by an almost endless range of flavourings. Cooks in every country have favourite flavour partnerships – chicken with saffron in a Spanish paella, hotly spiced for an Indian curry or in a stew with peanuts in the West Indies; turkey with a chilli and chocolate *mole* sauce in Mexico or with cranberry sauce in the USA; roast goose with apples in Germany or prunes in Scandinavia, or stuffed with potatoes in Ireland; duck with star anise in China, with pomegranates and walnuts in the Middle East or with horseradish sauce in Sweden; juniper-scented quail wrapped in vine leaves in France; guinea fowl with ginger and chestnuts in Poland; and pheasant with spiced cabbage in Eastern Europe or with bread sauce in the UK.

Here are some popular flavourings for poultry and game birds. All go well with the mild meat of chicken and turkey and most will also complement stronger-flavoured birds.

Pungent flavourings such as onions, shallots, garlic, fresh root ginger and chives.

Delicate herbs such as tarragon, basil, parsley (both curly and flat-leaf), coriander and chervil.

Robust herbs such as thyme, rosemary, lemon grass, bay leaf, marjoram, oregano and sage.

Warm spices such as juniper berries, allspice berries, star anise, cumin (seeds and ground) and caraway seeds.

Hot spices such as chillies (fresh, dried and ground), peppercorns (black, white, green and pink) and mustard (seeds and ground).

Fruit and nuts such as citrus (oranges, lemons and limes), mangoes, cranberries, cashews and chestnuts.

pungent flavourings

delicate herbs

robust herbs

warm spices

hot spices

fruit and nuts

Back to basics

Poultry and game birds are ideal for lower-fat cooking methods such as steaming, cooking en papillote, barbecuing, grilling, stir-frying, roasting, braising and pot-roasting. With well-flavoured stocks, made from the bones or giblets, and interesting, fibre-rich stuffings, you can create a wealth of healthy and delicious dishes.

Taking off the fat

Because most of the fat in many birds is in the skin, removing this before or after cooking is a good way to reduce the total fat content of a dish. When roasting, grilling or barbecuing, you can leave the skin on to keep the juices in during cooking, and then remove it before serving. If removing the skin before roasting or grilling, a steep in a marinade will help to keep a bird moist, as will regular basting.

Marinades

A marinade is a seasoned liquid used to flavour and tenderise as well as to add moisture. Game birds, particularly older ones that tend to be a bit tough and dry, benefit from a steep in a marinade for several hours, or even longer. Poultry, on the other hand, is more likely to be marinated briefly in a thicker mixture, often based on oil, vinegar, lemon juice, yogurt, herbs and spices.

Tips for lower-fat cooking

- Softened butter is often spread over the breast meat of poultry, under the skin, to add moisture. Fromage frais can be used in the same way, simply seasoned or mixed with herbs, citrus zest or other flavourings.

chicken stuffed under the skin

- Game birds are traditionally barded – the breast is covered with pork fat or streaky bacon – to compensate for the natural leanness of the breast meat. Back bacon rashers, stretched very thin, or Parma ham are good lower-fat substitutes for streaky bacon, but barding isn't necessary for game birds that are now intensively reared.
- If you put chicken or other poultry on a trivet in the roasting tin, it will prevent the bird from sitting in its own fat during roasting. It also allows fat to be poured away easily, before the meat juices are used to make a gravy or sauce.
- Placing a bird upside-down for the first half of the roasting time helps to keep the breast meat moist, and there is no need to baste with extra fat.
- Basting can be done with lemon juice or a small amount of oil rather than butter or other saturated fats, or you can use the juices released by the bird during cooking.
- After skimming most of the surface fat from the roasting juices, pour them into a gravy strainer, also called a gravy separator, which is a jug with a spout rising from the bottom. This allows you to pour off the juices, leaving behind the fat that is floating on the top.

a yogurt marinade adds flavour

Fresh chicken stock

A home-made stock is a far cry from over-seasoned cubes and pastes, and cheaper than the chilled stocks many supermarkets sell these days. This version, made with the leftovers from a roast chicken, can be used as a base for soups, casseroles, sauces and gravies.

Makes about 1 litre (1¾ pints)

1 chicken carcass or the bones from 4 chicken pieces

1 onion, quartered

1 large carrot, cut into large chunks

1 celery stick, cut into large chunks

1 fresh or 2 dried bay leaves

8 black peppercorns

½ tsp salt

Preparation time: 10 minutes

Cooking time: 2 hours

1 Break up the chicken carcass or bones and put into a large pan. Add the vegetables, bay leaves, peppercorns and salt. Pour over 2 litres (3½ pints) of water.

2 Bring to the boil over a high heat, then turn the heat down so the liquid is simmering gently. Cover the pan and leave to bubble for 2 hours.

3 Strain the stock through a sieve into a bowl, discarding the bones and vegetables. Skim the fat from the surface with a spoon, if using the stock straightaway. Alternatively, chill the stock first, which will make it easier to remove the fat.

Some more ideas

• If you don't have a chicken carcass or bones to hand, use 450 g (1 lb) chicken wings, which are extremely economical. Heat 1 tbsp of sunflower oil in a large pan and brown the wings (this will give a richer flavour and colour to the stock). Add the rest of the ingredients and cook as above.

• You can make the stock from a raw chicken carcass or bones. When bringing to the boil, skim off all the scum that rises to the surface, then leave to simmer.

• For a stronger flavour, boil the strained stock rapidly, without a lid, to reduce the quantity.

• For a giblet stock, put the giblets (gizzard, heart and neck, but not the liver, which can give a bitter flavour) in a pan with 1 quartered unpeeled onion, 1 roughly chopped carrot and 1 chopped celery stick. Add a bouquet garni of 1 bay leaf, a few parsley stalks and a sprig of fresh thyme, tied together, and a few black peppercorns. Cover with cold water and bring to the boil, skimming off any scum. Then reduce the heat and simmer for 1 hour. Strain, cool quickly and refrigerate.

• Use the carcass of a turkey or other bird, rather than chicken.

Stuffings for poultry

Packed with flavour and texture, these stuffings are also low in fat and high in fibre and carbohydrate. Stuffed into a bird, or baked alongside, they enable you to serve smaller portions of meat – with lots of vegetables – which means your meal will be in the right, healthy proportions. If you have a large bird, just increase the quantities for all these stuffings.

Apple, walnut and prune stuffing

Serves 6

100 g (3½ oz) pitted Agen prunes
3 tbsp port or fresh orange juice
1 small dessert apple, cored and finely chopped
2 shallots, finely chopped
30 g (1 oz) walnut pieces, coarsely chopped
75 g (2½ oz) fresh Granary breadcrumbs
1–2 tbsp fresh thyme leaves
1 egg, beaten
salt and pepper

Preparation time: 15 minutes
Cooking time: 20 or 40 minutes,
    depending upon method used

1 Snip the prunes into small chunks using scissors. Place in a small saucepan and add the port or orange juice. Set over a low heat and bring almost to the boil, by which time the prunes will have absorbed the liquid and become plump. Spoon into a mixing bowl.
2 Add the apple and shallots and stir. Add the walnuts, breadcrumbs, thyme, egg and seasoning, and mix thoroughly.
3 Stuff into the neck end of a chicken or turkey, shaping any leftover stuffing into walnut-sized balls to cook separately. If you have made stuffing balls, arrange them on a lightly oiled baking tray and put into the oven for the last 20 minutes of the bird's cooking time.
4 Alternatively, put all of the stuffing into a lightly greased ovenproof dish, about 17.5 cm (7 in) in diameter, spreading it out evenly and packing it down. Bake in a preheated oven at 200°C (400°F, gas mark 6) for 40 minutes.

Another idea

• Instead of prunes, soak chopped ready-to-eat dried apricots in Armagnac and mix with almonds in place of walnuts, and 2 celery sticks, finely chopped, instead of apple. Season with 1 tsp ground cinnamon and ½ tsp freshly grated nutmeg.

Sausage and chestnut stuffing

Serves 6

100 g (3½ oz) premium high-meat-content pork sausages

100 g (3½ oz) cooked or vacuum-packed chestnuts, finely chopped

2 shallots, finely chopped

75 g (2½ oz) fresh breadcrumbs

1½ tbsp chopped fresh sage

1 egg, beaten

salt and pepper

Preparation time: 10 minutes

Cooking time: 30 or 40 minutes, depending upon method used

1 Remove the sausage meat from the skins and put into a bowl. Add the chopped chestnuts and shallots and mix into the sausage meat. Add the breadcrumbs, sage, egg and some seasoning and mix thoroughly.

2 Stuff into the neck end of a chicken or turkey, shaping any leftover stuffing into walnut-sized balls to cook separately. If you have made stuffing balls, arrange them on a lightly oiled baking tray and put into the oven for the last 30 minutes of the bird's cooking time.

3 Alternatively, put all of the stuffing into a lightly greased ovenproof dish, about 17.5 cm (7 in) in diameter, spreading it out evenly and packing it down. Bake in a preheated oven at 200°C (400°F, gas mark 6) for 40 minutes.

Some more ideas

● Substitute canned unsweetened chestnut purée for the chopped chestnuts.

● Use wholemeal breadcrumbs to boost the fibre content.

● For a simple sage and onion stuffing, chop 3 medium-sized onions and cook in 30 g (1 oz) butter until soft and golden. Transfer to a bowl and add 170 g (6 oz) fresh breadcrumbs, 2 tbsp chopped fresh sage or 2 tsp crumbled dried sage, 1 beaten egg and seasoning to taste.

Poultry First

Flavoursome soups and starters

Poultry not only offers health benefits, but also great economy. Whatever the bird, almost every bit can be used. Simmer the bones for stock, then try a turkey soup with lots of vegetables, chestnuts and pearl barley, or a hearty chicken and sweetcorn chowder, or a tasty pheasant, wild rice and mushroom broth. Combine turkey livers with lentils in a coarse-textured pâté, or transform chicken livers into a smooth and elegant mousse. For a special occasion make a delectable duck terrine and serve it with a zesty salsa. Roll chicken in filo, or grill it on skewers and serve with a peanut sauce. Or try an exotic South-east Asian soup spiced with aromatic lemongrass.

Turkey, chestnut and barley broth

When you roast a turkey, don't throw away the carcass. Instead, use it to make this wonderfully rich-tasting soup. Reminiscent of an Italian minestrone, it is packed with vegetables, barley, turkey meat and chestnuts – a really satisfying bowl of soup. Serve with warm, crusty wholegrain bread.

Serves 6

Stock

1 roast turkey carcass

1 onion, cut into quarters

1 carrot, chopped

2 celery sticks, chopped

few sprigs of parsley

few sprigs of fresh thyme

1 bay leaf

Soup

1 large carrot, chopped

1 large parsnip, chopped

3 celery sticks, chopped

4–6 Brussels sprouts, chopped

1 large leek, chopped

100 g (3½ oz) freshly cooked or vacuum-packed chestnuts, roughly chopped

75 g (2½ oz) pearl barley

3 tbsp chopped parsley

100 g (3½ oz) cooked turkey meat, without skin, chopped or shredded

salt and pepper

Preparation time: 15 minutes

Cooking time: about 2¼ hours

Each serving provides

kcal 115, **protein** 7 g, **fat** 1.2 g (of which saturated fat 0.2 g), **carbohydrate** 20 g (of which sugars 3.5 g), **fibre** 2 g

✓ B₆, C, E, folate

1 First, make the stock. Break up the turkey carcass, discarding any skin, and place in a very large saucepan. Add the quartered onion, carrot and celery. Tie the herb sprigs and bay leaf into a bouquet garni and add to the pan. Cover generously with water and bring to the boil, skimming any scum from the surface with a draining spoon. Reduce the heat, cover the pan and simmer gently for 1½ hours. Strain the stock, and discard the bones and vegetables.

2 Measure the stock and, if necessary, make up to 1.7 litres (3 pints) with water. Skim off any fat and pour back into the cleaned saucepan.

3 Bring the stock back to the boil. Add the chopped vegetables, chestnuts and pearl barley, and simmer for 35 minutes or until the pearl barley is tender.

4 Add the parsley and turkey, and heat through thoroughly. Season with salt and pepper and serve.

Plus points

• Barley is believed to be the world's oldest cultivated grain. It is low in fat and rich in starchy carbohydrate. It contains traces of gluten, but is useful for those on wheat-free diets.

• Celery provides potassium and also acts as a diuretic, helping to reduce fluid and salt retention.

• Unlike other nuts, chestnuts are high in complex carbohydrates and low in fat – Brazil nuts, hazelnuts and walnuts have 20 times as much fat as chestnuts. Chestnuts also provide useful amounts of vitamins E and B₆.

Another idea

• For a turkey, lentil and sweet potato soup, add red lentils instead of pearl barley and use 1 large orange-fleshed sweet potato, 1 large parsnip and 225 g (8 oz) celeriac instead of the carrot, parsnip, celery, sprouts and leek. Flavour the soup with 1 tbsp redcurrant jelly, stirred in just before serving.

poultry first

Chicken and sweetcorn chowder

This hearty soup tastes really special, yet despite its creamy texture it doesn't contain any cream. Made with cooked chicken and fresh sweetcorn and potatoes, with a garnish of grilled back bacon, it's substantial enough for a light lunch, served with crusty bread and followed by salad or fruit.

Serves 4

3 fresh corn-on-the-cob

2 tbsp sunflower oil

1 onion, finely chopped

2 potatoes, about 300 g (10½ oz) in total, peeled and diced

500 ml (17 fl oz) chicken stock, preferably home-made (see page 23)

500 ml (17 fl oz) semi-skimmed milk

250 g (9 oz) cooked chicken meat, without skin, finely chopped

2 tsp chopped fresh tarragon

salt and pepper

To garnish

2 rashers lean smoked back bacon

fresh tarragon leaves

Preparation time: 15 minutes

Cooking time: 25 minutes

Each serving provides

kcal 320, **protein** 26 g, **fat** 12 g (of which saturated fat 3.5 g), **carbohydrate** 27 g (of which sugars 7.5 g), **fibre** 1.5 g

✓✓	B$_6$, E, calcium
✓	B$_1$, B$_2$, B$_{12}$, C, folate, niacin, copper, iron, potassium, zinc

1 Remove the green husks and all the 'silk' from the corn. Holding each cob upright on a chopping board, cut the kernels from the cob. You should end up with 225–250 g (8–9 oz) loose corn kernels. Set the kernels aside.

2 Heat the sunflower oil in a large saucepan, add the onion and fry over a moderate heat until softened, but not browned. Add the potatoes and sweetcorn kernels to the pan and cook for a further 5 minutes, stirring frequently. Pour in the chicken stock and bring to the boil. Reduce the heat and simmer gently for 5 minutes or until the potatoes are just tender.

3 Stir in the milk, three-quarters of the chicken and the chopped tarragon. Season to taste. Cook, stirring, for a further 2–3 minutes.

4 Pour half of the mixture into a food processor or blender and blend to a coarse texture, not to a purée. Return to the pan. Add the rest of the chicken and stir to mix. Set the chowder over a low heat to warm through.

5 Meanwhile, grill the rashers of bacon until cooked and starting to brown. Drain the bacon on kitchen paper, then finely chop.

6 Ladle the chowder into bowls, scatter on some bacon and a sprinkling of tarragon leaves, and serve.

Plus points

• Milk is an excellent source of many important nutrients, including protein, calcium and many of the B vitamins.

• Sweetcorn is a useful source of dietary fibre, important for keeping the digestive system in good working order, and also offers vitamin C and folate.

• Bacon, like other meat, provides iron, plus vitamin B$_1$, essential for maintaining a healthy nervous system.

poultry first

Some more ideas

- Use 225 g (8 oz) frozen sweetcorn instead of fresh kernels cut from the cob. Thaw and drain them before adding. Alternatively, if more convenient, you can use a 190 g or 340 g can of sweetcorn (preferably without added sugar), drained, depending on how much sweetcorn you like in your soup.
- Substitute a large leek, sliced, for the onion.
- For a creamy chicken soup with mushrooms, use 100 g (3½ oz) chestnut mushrooms, finely chopped, instead of the sweetcorn and potato. Add 1 tablespoon Madeira after cooking the mushrooms for 5 minutes and leave to bubble to evaporate most of it before pouring in the stock. Blend a little of the milk with 1 heaped tbsp of plain flour until smooth, then stir in the remaining milk and add to the pan with the chicken and tarragon. Cook, stirring, until thickened. Mushrooms are a good source of potassium.
- Instead of bacon, garnish the soup with croutons: cut 55 g (2 oz) crustless bread into small cubes and stir in a bowl with 1 tbsp sunflower oil. Spread out on a baking tray and bake in a preheated oven at 180°C (350°F, gas mark 4) for 10 minutes or until golden. Toss the baked croutons with 1 tsp very finely chopped fresh tarragon, if you like. These baked croutons are far less fatty than croutons fried in oil. For garlic croutons, toss the bread cubes in 1 tbsp olive oil mixed with a crushed garlic clove before baking them.

poultry first

31

Pheasant broth with wild rice

If you've roasted a brace of pheasants – traditionally a hen and a cock – then it is simplicity itself to transform the carcasses into this deliciously tasty and nutritious soup. With nutty rice grains, tender mushrooms and herbs, it makes a perfect starter before a light main dish.

Serves 4

2 tbsp extra virgin olive oil

1 onion, quartered

1 large carrot, about 115 g (4 oz), thickly sliced

1 celery stick, thickly sliced

1 large sprig of parsley

1 sprig of fresh thyme

2 bay leaves

2 garlic cloves, halved

150 ml (5 fl oz) red wine

2 cooked pheasant carcasses

55 g (2 oz) mixed wild rice and brown rice

15 g (½ oz) dried porcini mushrooms

115 g (4 oz) chestnut mushrooms, thinly sliced

pinch of freshly grated nutmeg

salt and pepper

To garnish

finely shredded zest of ½ orange

fresh thyme leaves

Preparation time: 10 minutes, plus chilling overnight

Cooking time: 2 hours 50 minutes

Each serving provides

kcal 165, **protein** 3 g, **fat** 6 g (of which saturated fat 1 g), **carbohydrate** 19.5 g (of which sugars 6 g), **fibre** 2 g

✓✓	E, copper
✓	B$_6$

1 Heat 1 tbsp of the oil in a large saucepan and add the onion, carrot and celery. Cook, stirring occasionally, for 5–6 minutes or until browned. Tie the parsley, thyme and bay leaves together into a bouquet garni and add to the pan with the garlic and red wine. Boil rapidly for 1 minute.

2 Cut any meat from the pheasant carcasses and reserve. Break up the carcasses, then add to the saucepan together with 2 litres (3½ pints) of cold water. Bring to the boil, then reduce the heat and simmer for 2 hours. Strain the stock and refrigerate overnight.

3 Skim off any fat from the stock, then bring to the boil and cook rapidly for 15–20 minutes or until it has reduced to 1.2 litres (2 pints). Add the rice and reserved pheasant meat and stir well, then reduce the heat and simmer for 30 minutes or until the rice grains are just tender.

4 Meanwhile, pour boiling water over the dried porcini mushrooms and soak for 20 minutes to rehydrate. Lift them out of the soaking water, dry on kitchen paper and chop finely. Heat the remaining 1 tbsp oil in a sauté pan and cook the chestnut mushrooms over a moderate heat for 3 minutes or until lightly golden. Add the porcini and cook for a further 1 minute.

5 When the rice is tender, add the cooked mushrooms and season with nutmeg and salt and pepper to taste. Serve hot, garnishing each bowl of soup with a few shreds of orange zest and thyme leaves.

Plus points

• Unlike white rice, brown rice still contains the germ and bran of the rice grain and therefore offers more fibre and higher levels of the B vitamins than white rice.

• Mushrooms contain the B vitamins B$_2$, niacin and pantothenic acid, and they provide potassium as well as good quantities of copper.

• Wild rice is not true rice but the seeds of a North American wild aquatic grass. Like rice it is gluten-free. It contains useful amounts of the B vitamins, particularly niacin, and dietary fibre.

Some more ideas

• For a pheasant and lentil variation of this soup, add 1 tbsp crushed juniper berries with the wine when making the pheasant stock. After boiling the strained stock to reduce to 1.2 litres (2 pints), add 55 g (2 oz) green lentils and simmer for 30 minutes or until the lentils are just tender. Then add 12 freshly cooked or vacuum-packed chestnuts, chopped, and 1 finely sliced leek. Cover and simmer for a further 10 minutes or until the leek is tender. Garnish with celery leaves. Unlike other nuts, chestnuts are high in complex carbohydrates and low in fat.

• Using poultry carcasses to make stock is a great way to get all the goodness left in the bones. If you don't have time to make stock into a soup right away, boil to reduce it (as in step 3) and then freeze it. Use it as a base for sauces or other soups at a more convenient time.

Duck goulash soup

Duck legs make a richly flavoured, hearty goulash soup – the meat is delicious spooned up with the chunks of carrot, celeriac and mushroom, and a spoonful of soured cream gives a creamy finish. For a complete meal in a bowl, add some potato dumplings flavoured with onion and garlic (see 'Some more ideas' opposite).

Serves 6

3 duck leg joints, about 375 g (13 oz) each, skinned

2 tbsp sunflower oil

250 ml (8½ fl oz) dry white wine

2 onions, chopped

2 garlic cloves, coarsely chopped

2 peppers, 1 red and 1 green, seeded and diced

1 large carrot, diced

125 g (4½ oz) celeriac, peeled and diced

2 tbsp paprika

¼ tsp caraway seeds

1½ tbsp plain flour

1 bay leaf

900 ml (1½ pints) chicken stock, preferably home-made (see page 23)

450 g (1 lb) tomatoes, diced

15 g (½ oz) mixed dried mushrooms, rinsed well to remove all grit, then chopped

100 g (3½ oz) fresh mushrooms, sliced

pinch of cayenne pepper

2 tbsp chopped parsley

salt and pepper

To serve

6 tbsp soured cream or Greek-style yogurt

chopped parsley

Preparation time: 30 minutes

Cooking time: 1½ hours

1 Sprinkle the duck legs with salt and pepper. Heat 1 tsp of the oil in a heavy-based non-stick frying pan, add the duck legs and brown on both sides. Remove from the pan and set aside. Add the wine and boil for 5 minutes or until it is reduced by about half. Remove from the heat and reserve.

2 Heat the remaining oil in a large saucepan. Add the onions and garlic, and sauté for 5 minutes or until the onions are softened. Add the red and green peppers, carrot and celeriac, and cook for 5 more minutes. Stir in the paprika and caraway seeds, and cook for a minute or two, then add the flour and stir to coat the vegetables. Cook, stirring, for 2–3 minutes.

3 Add the bay leaf, chicken stock, reserved wine mixture, tomatoes, dried and fresh mushrooms, cayenne pepper and parsley. Stir well to mix. Add the duck legs. Bring to the boil, then reduce the heat to low, cover and simmer for about 1 hour or until the duck is tender.

4 Remove the duck legs from the soup. Take the meat off the bones in large shreds. Return the meat to the soup. Check the seasoning.

5 Ladle the soup into bowls. Garnish each with a spoonful of soured cream or yogurt and some parsley.

Plus points

- Tomatoes contain lycopene, a carotenoid compound that acts as an antioxidant. Recent studies suggest that lycopene may help to protect against bladder and pancreatic cancers.

- Skinning duck before cooking removes about two-thirds of the fat.

- Duck is a good source of many of the B vitamins, as well as providing iron and zinc. Weight for weight, it contains over twice as much B_1 and B_2 as chicken and 3 times as much iron.

Each serving provides

kcal 255, **protein** 16 g, **fat** 11 g (of which saturated fat 3.5 g), **carbohydrate** 17 g (of which sugars 10 g), **fibre** 4 g

✓✓✓	A, B_6, B_{12}, C
✓✓	B_1, B_2, E, folate, copper, iron, zinc
✓	potassium

poultry first

Some more ideas

• For a duck and cabbage goulash soup, blanch ½ head of shredded green cabbage in boiling salted water until it is just wilted. Drain well, then add to the simmering soup about halfway through the cooking time in step 3.

• To make potato dumplings for the soup, use 750 g (1 lb 10 oz) floury potatoes, such as King Edwards, cut in half if large. Cook them in boiling salted water until tender, but not soft and mushy. Drain well and leave until cool enough to handle, then peel. Mash or grate coarsely. Add 1 egg, lightly beaten, 1 tbsp semi-skimmed milk, 4 tbsp each plain flour and couscous, 2 spring onions, thinly sliced, 2 chopped garlic cloves, and salt and pepper to taste, then mix to a dough. Take a lump of the dough, about 2 tbsp, and roll into a tight ball.

Repeat to make 12 dumplings in all. Bring a wide pan of water to the boil. Gently plop the dumplings into the water and let the water come to the boil again, then lower the heat until the water is gently simmering and cook for 10–12 minutes. Lift out the dumplings with a draining spoon and leave them to drain on kitchen paper for a few minutes. Add 2 dumplings to each bowl of goulash soup and serve.

Chicken with lemongrass

A cross between a soup and stew, this dish captures the exciting spicy and sour flavours of South-east Asia. Lemongrass gives a citrus touch, and creamed coconut – using just the minimum for flavour – adds richness without excessive fat. Using the poaching liquid as the broth preserves the water-soluble vitamins.

Serves 4

1 small fresh red chilli, such as bird's-eye, split open lengthways but left whole

1 garlic clove, cut in half

1 cm (½ in) piece fresh root ginger, peeled and cut into 4 slices

2 stalks lemongrass, bruised and cut in half

4 chicken joints, such as breasts or thighs, about 170 g (6 oz) each, skinned

1 shallot, finely chopped

250 g (9 oz) fine French beans, trimmed and cut into bite-sized pieces

1 courgette, sliced lengthways with a vegetable peeler into thin strips

75 g (2½ oz) creamed coconut, crumbled

finely grated zest and juice of 1 lime

2 tbsp chopped fresh coriander

salt and pepper

Preparation time: about 25 minutes, plus 30 minutes infusing

Cooking time: about 25 minutes

Each serving provides

kcal 325, **protein** 35.5 g, **fat** 18 g (of which saturated fat 13 g), **carbohydrate** 5 g (of which sugars 4 g), **fibre** 2 g

✓✓✓ B$_6$

✓✓ B$_1$, B$_2$, C, folate, niacin, copper, iron, potassium, zinc

1 Place 1 litre (1¾ pints) water in a saucepan over a high heat. Spear the chilli, garlic and ginger on a wooden cocktail stick (this makes them easy to remove later) and add to the pan together with the lemongrass. Bring to the boil and boil for 1 minute, then remove from the heat, cover and set aside to infuse for 30 minutes.

2 Return the liquid to the boil, then reduce the heat to low. Add the chicken joints, shallot and French beans, and poach for 12–15 minutes or until the chicken is cooked (test with the tip of a knife: the juices should run clear). Add the courgette slices for the last 2 minutes of cooking.

3 Using a draining spoon, transfer the chicken, beans and courgettes to a warmed bowl. Add a little of the poaching liquid to keep them moist, then cover tightly and keep warm.

4 Return the liquid to the boil and add the creamed coconut, stirring until it dissolves. Continue boiling for 5–6 minutes or until the liquid has reduced by about one-third.

5 Remove the chicken meat from the bones and shred it roughly. Return the chicken meat, beans and courgettes to the soup and stir, then reheat briefly. Stir in the grated lime zest and juice. Season to taste.

6 Divide the chicken and vegetables among 4 soup plates. Spoon over the liquid, discarding the lemongrass and stick of chilli, garlic and ginger. Sprinkle with the coriander and serve.

Some more ideas

• To turn this into a more filling dish, add some noodles. Soak 100 g (3½ oz) Chinese egg noodles in boiling water for 3 minutes, or according to the packet instructions, then drain. Stir into the reduced cooking liquid with the chicken and vegetables in step 5.

• Replace the green beans with asparagus tips, adding them with the courgettes. Also add 225 g (8 oz) frozen peas, straight from the freezer, after dissolving the creamed coconut.

• Tiny red bird's-eye chilli is fiery-hot. To reduce the heat in this dish, seed the chilli, remove it after the liquid infuses, or replace it with a milder red chilli or a green one.

Plus points

• French beans are a good source of the B vitamin folate, essential for a healthy pregnancy. It is important to ensure a good intake of folate in the early stages of pregnancy to prevent spina bifida. Folate may also have a role in helping to protect against heart disease.

Duck terrine and ginger-plum salsa

The distinctive duck flavour of this terrine, heightened by the hint of orange, is perfectly complemented by the sweet leeks and fresh green beans. A small amount of duck fat is included, but there is still much less fat than would be found in a traditional recipe. This terrine will keep in the fridge for up to 4 days.

Serves 8

300 g (10½ oz) boneless duck breasts

1 tbsp extra virgin olive oil

400 g (14 oz) leeks, thinly sliced

2 garlic cloves, crushed

1 orange

a few fresh bay leaves

55 g (2 oz) French beans, trimmed

1 tbsp chopped fresh thyme

1 tbsp brandy

salt and pepper

orange slices or segments to garnish

Ginger-plum salsa

450 g (1 lb) ripe dessert plums, stoned and
 finely chopped

1 piece preserved stem ginger, finely chopped

2 tbsp orange juice

freshly grated nutmeg

Preparation time: 30 minutes, plus cooling and
 at least 12 hours chilling

Cooking time: 1½ hours

Each serving provides

kcal 100, **protein** 9 g, **fat** 4 g (of which saturated fat 1 g), **carbohydrate** 7.5 g (of which sugars 7 g), **fibre** 2 g

✓✓✓	B$_{12}$
✓✓	B$_6$, C
✓	A, B$_1$, folate, copper, iron, potassium

1 Remove the skin and fat from the duck breasts. Reserve 30 g (1 oz) of the fat, and discard the remainder together with the skin. Chop the meat. Set aside.

2 Heat the oil in a large saucepan over a moderate heat. Stir in the leeks and garlic, then reduce the heat to low, cover and cook for 20 minutes.

3 Meanwhile, preheat the oven to 180°C (350°F, gas mark 4). Line the bottom of a 450 g (1 lb) loaf tin with greaseproof paper. Finely grate the zest from the orange and set aside. Peel the orange, then cut half of it into slices; chop the other half and keep for the salsa. Decoratively arrange the bay leaves and orange slices on the bottom of the tin. Set aside.

4 Bring a saucepan of water to the boil. Add the beans and, when the water returns to the boil, blanch for 2 minutes. Drain and refresh under cold water. Pat dry and set aside.

5 Place the chopped duck breasts, reserved duck fat, orange zest, thyme and brandy in a food processor and pulse until well blended to a paste-like consistency. When the leeks have finished cooking, add them to the processor and pulse again once or twice, but do not blend them in too much. Season with a little salt and pepper.

6 Spoon half of the duck mixture into the prepared loaf tin, taking care not to disturb the orange slices and bay leaves. Pack down and smooth the surface. Arrange the beans in a single layer on top, laying them lengthways. Top with the remaining duck mixture and smooth the surface.

7 Cover the loaf tin with foil. Place it in a roasting tin and pour in enough hot water to come halfway up the side of the loaf tin. Bake for 1½ hours or until the juices run clear when the terrine is pierced with a knife.

8 Remove the loaf tin from the roasting tin. Place a piece of card, cut to fit, directly on top of the terrine and weight it down. Leave until cold, then chill for at least 12 hours.

9 To make the salsa, put the plums into a bowl with the ginger, orange juice and nutmeg to taste. Add the reserved chopped orange. Cover and chill until 15 minutes before serving.

10 To serve, run a round-bladed knife down the sides of the terrine, then invert it onto a serving platter. Peel off the lining paper. Allow the terrine to come to room temperature before cutting into slices. Serve each slice of terrine garnished with orange and accompanied with a portion of salsa and toast or French bread.

Some more ideas

- For a spicier salsa, replace the ginger with 1 fresh red chilli, seeded and finely chopped, or to taste. Instead of the nutmeg, add 1 tbsp finely chopped fresh coriander just before serving.
- A delicious citrus salsa, packed with vitamin C, can be made by mixing 1 large grapefruit and 1 large orange, both peeled and finely chopped, with 2 spring onions, very finely chopped, 1 fresh green chilli, seeded and finely chopped, and 2 tbsp finely chopped fresh coriander or parsley.
- To make a chicken terrine, replace the duck breasts with skinless boneless chicken thighs and use 30 g (1 oz) rindless streaky bacon instead of the duck fat. This terrine is very good with the citrus salsa above.

Plus points

- The plums and orange juice in the salsa provide vitamin C, which helps to increase the absorption of iron from the duck.
- This terrine is an excellent source of vitamin B_{12}, important for the formation of red blood cells. It is also low in fat, most of which is unsaturated.

poultry first

39

Turkey and lentil pâté

This coarse-textured pâté, deliciously flavoured with garlic and fresh coriander, combines minced turkey and turkey livers with lentils for a starter that has considerably less fat than a traditional pâté. Serve with toasted slices of brioche or other bread, plus some crisp vegetable sticks and crunchy radishes.

Serves 6

55 g (2 oz) green lentils

1½ tbsp sunflower oil

4 shallots, finely chopped

1 garlic clove, crushed

450 g (1 lb) minced turkey

115 g (4 oz) turkey livers, chopped

3 tbsp dry Marsala wine

30 g (1 oz) fresh coriander leaves

salt and pepper

sprigs of fresh coriander to garnish

Preparation time: 1¼ hours, plus about 2 hours chilling

Each serving provides

kcal 245, **protein** 33 g, **fat** 9 g (of which saturated fat 2.5 g), **carbohydrate** 6 g (of which sugars 1 g), **fibre** 1 g

✓✓✓	A, B$_2$, B$_6$, B$_{12}$, folate, niacin, iron
✓✓	B$_1$, C, copper, zinc
✓	E, potassium, selenium

1 Put the lentils in a saucepan, cover generously with water and bring to the boil. Simmer for about 45 minutes or until tender. Drain well and set aside to cool.

2 Heat the oil in a large frying pan and fry the shallots and garlic over a moderately high heat for 2 minutes or until they have softened. Reduce the heat to moderate and add the minced turkey and the livers. Cook, stirring, for 8–10 minutes.

3 Pour in the Marsala, bring to the boil and allow the mixture to bubble for 1–2 minutes. Season with salt and pepper.

4 Transfer the mixture to a food processor. Add the coriander leaves and cooked lentils, and process for a few seconds to form a coarse paste consistency. Alternatively, chop the coriander finely, and mash all the ingredients together thoroughly using a fork.

5 Spoon into 6 ramekins, pressing down well with the back of the spoon. Cover and chill for about 2 hours before serving, garnished with fresh coriander sprigs.

Plus points

● Turkey livers are a rich source of iron, zinc, vitamin A and many of the B vitamins, especially B$_{12}$. The iron present in the livers is in a form that is easily absorbed by the human body.

● As well as providing fibre, lentils are a good source of vitamins B$_1$ and niacin, essential for efficient energy metabolism.

Some more ideas

● Use chicken livers instead of turkey livers, or a mixture of the two.

● Replace the Marsala with medium sherry.

● For a turkey and apricot pâté, omit the lentils and instead use 55 g (2 oz) dried apricots, diced, and 115 g (4 oz) mushrooms, finely chopped. Cook with the minced turkey and livers in step 2. Replace the Marsala with 2 tbsp brandy. Dried apricots are a useful source of vitamin A (through beta-carotene) and one of the richest fruit sources of iron.

Chicken liver mousse

A splash of brandy makes this light and smooth mousse special enough for a dinner party first course. Poaching the chicken livers with vegetables and herbs, instead of frying them, gives them lots of flavour, and fromage frais adds the richness that would traditionally be added by butter, but without the saturated fat.

Serves 4

250 g (9 oz) chicken livers, well trimmed
1 onion, finely chopped
1 garlic clove, crushed
600 ml (1 pint) vegetable stock or water
several sprigs of parsley
several sprigs of fresh thyme
1 bay leaf
1–1½ tbsp fromage frais
2 tsp garlic vinegar or white wine vinegar
2 tsp brandy or Calvados, or to taste
1 tbsp pink or green peppercorns in brine, drained and patted dry
2 tbsp finely chopped parsley
salt and pepper

Preparation time: 10 minutes, plus at least 4 hours chilling
Cooking time: about 15 minutes

Each serving provides

kcal 80, protein 12.5 g, fat 1.5 g (of which saturated fat 0.4 g), carbohydrate 3.5 g (of which sugars 2.5 g), fibre 1 g

✓✓✓	A, B$_2$, B$_6$, B$_{12}$, folate, iron
✓✓	C, copper, zinc
✓	B$_1$, niacin

1 Place the chicken livers, onion and garlic in a saucepan and add stock or water to cover. Tie the parsley, thyme and bay leaf into a bouquet garni and add to the pan. Slowly bring to the boil, skimming the surface as necessary, then reduce the heat and simmer gently for 5–8 minutes or until the livers are cooked through but still slightly pink in the centre when you cut into one.

2 Drain, and discard the bouquet garni. Tip the livers, onions and garlic into a food processor. Add 1 tbsp of the fromage frais, the vinegar and brandy, and process until smooth, adding the remaining ½ tbsp fromage frais if it is necessary for a lighter texture. Season to taste, then stir in the peppercorns. Alternatively, tip the livers, onions and garlic into a bowl and mash with a fork to a slightly coarse paste. Add the fromage frais, vinegar and brandy and mix well, then season and stir in the peppercorns.

3 Spoon the mousse into a serving bowl, or individual ramekins, and smooth the top. Sprinkle with a layer of finely chopped parsley. Cover with cling film and chill for at least 4 hours, but preferably overnight.

4 Before serving, allow the mousse to return to room temperature. Serve with slices of hot toast.

Some more ideas

● Replace the brandy with orange juice and add the finely grated zest of ½ orange.
● If you can't find pink or green peppercorns, substitute finely chopped drained capers.
● For a smooth mousse, made without a food processor, omit the onion, and sieve the cooked livers and garlic. Add 2 spring onions, finely chopped, with the peppercorns.
● For a less rich mousse to serve 6, omit the brandy and add 100 g (3½ oz) drained canned cannellini beans, rinsed and dried, to the food processor with ½ tbsp finely chopped fresh sage. This mousse is excellent on toasted slices of country-style bread, or spread on slices of baguette and then topped with sliced gherkins.
● Vary the herbs – chopped fresh chives, tarragon and mint all go well with chicken liver mousse.

Plus points

● Chicken livers are one of the richest sources of iron – each serving of this mousse provides more than half of the recommended daily intake.
● Many traditional recipes for chicken liver mousse and pâté seal the surface with a layer of melted or clarified butter for storage. In this version the fat is replaced by the chopped fresh herbs.

Chicken satay

Moist, gingery cubes of chicken breast and colourful crunchy vegetables are grilled on traditional wooden skewers and served with a peanut sauce in this version of the popular Indonesian snack. Wedges of lime are included on the skewers so the hot juice can be squeezed over the cooked chicken just before eating.

Serves 4

2 cm (¾ in) piece fresh root ginger, peeled and finely chopped

2 tbsp soy sauce

juice of ½ lime

1 tbsp sunflower oil

340 g (12 oz) skinless boneless chicken breasts (fillets), cut into 2 cm (¾ in) cubes

1 lime, cut into 8 wedges

8 cherry tomatoes, about 100 g (3½ oz) in total

1 yellow pepper, seeded and cut into chunky pieces

1 courgette, about 150 g (5½ oz), thickly sliced

sprigs of fresh coriander to garnish

Peanut sauce

2 tsp sunflower oil

1 small onion, finely chopped

50 g (1¾ oz) unsalted peanuts, finely chopped

1 garlic clove, chopped

1 tsp green Thai curry paste

1 tbsp soy sauce

½ tsp caster sugar

25 g (scant 1 oz) creamed coconut

Preparation time: 40 minutes, plus at least 2 hours marinating

Cooking time: 10–15 minutes

1 To make the marinade, mix the ginger, soy sauce, lime juice and oil together in a bowl. Add the chicken and toss to coat. Cover with cling film and leave to marinate in the fridge for at least 2 hours, turning once or twice.

2 Soak 8 wooden skewers in cold water for at least 30 minutes.

3 Meanwhile, make the peanut sauce. Heat the oil in a small saucepan, add the onion and cook over a moderate heat, stirring, for 3 minutes. Add the peanuts and cook for 3–5 minutes or until both the nuts and onion are lightly browned, stirring occasionally. Add the garlic, curry paste, soy sauce, sugar and 150 ml (5 fl oz) of water. Bring to the boil. Crumble in the creamed coconut and stir until dissolved. Simmer gently for 5 minutes or until thickened, stirring occasionally. Purée the sauce in a blender or food processor to make a thick cream. Return to the saucepan and set aside.

4 Preheat the grill to high. Lift the chicken out of the marinade; reserve the marinade. Thread the chicken, lime wedges and vegetables onto the soaked skewers. Arrange the skewers on the grill rack and brush with the marinade. Place under the grill, close to the heat, and cook for 10–15 minutes, turning once or twice, until the ingredients are browned and the chicken is cooked thoroughly. Test by cutting one of the chicken pieces in half with a knife; there should be no hint of pink.

5 While the satay is cooking, reheat the sauce. Arrange the satay on 4 serving plates, garnish with sprigs of coriander and serve with the sauce.

Plus points

• In common with most other nuts, peanuts are high in fat, although much of the fat they contain is of the unsaturated variety. New research suggests that diets which contain a daily intake of peanuts, peanut butter or peanut (groundnut) oil may help to lower total cholesterol, particularly harmful LDL cholesterol, and thus help to protect against coronary heart disease.

Each serving provides

kcal 313, **protein** 26 g, **fat** 19.5 g (of which saturated fat 6 g), **carbohydrate** 8 g (of which sugars 6.5 g), **fibre** 2.5 g

✓✓✓	B₆, C, E
✓✓	niacin
✓	folate, copper, iron, potassium, selenium, zinc

poultry first

44

Some more ideas

- If you have young children in your family, you may prefer to make up half the marinade and use it for adult portions only. For the children, thread plain chicken onto skewers and brush with a little sunflower oil before grilling.
- A 250 g (9 oz) pack of firm tofu could be used to replace half of the chicken, thus reducing the saturated fat content – or you could use all tofu for a vegetarian dish. Drain the tofu well, cut it into large cubes and marinate with the chicken.
- Quorn is another vegetarian option which can replace some or all of the chicken.
- Try other vegetable combinations, such as 1 red onion, cut into 8 wedges, 8 medium-sized button mushrooms, about 100 g (3½ oz) in total, and 50 g (1¾ oz) mange-touts.
- To make this into a main dish, use 450 g (1 lb) chicken. Serve the satay on a bed of Thai fragrant rice and accompany with a salad of sliced cucumber tossed with a little white wine vinegar and a few drops of mild or medium chilli sauce.

poultry first

Vietnamese-style pigeon parcels

In authentic Vietnamese parcels, the mixture would be wrapped in rice paper and then deep-fried. This recipe saves on the fat by poaching the pigeon mixture in a flavourful broth, and then wrapping the parcels in lettuce leaves – Little Gem or round lettuce – with fresh herbs. The result is very attractive and fun to eat.

Serves 4 (makes 16)

Pigeon rolls

225 g (8 oz) skinless boneless pigeon breasts, roughly chopped

1 small carrot, coarsely grated

55 g (2 oz) shiitake mushrooms, chopped

2 spring onions, roughly chopped

30 g (1 oz) rice noodles, soaked in hot water for 5 minutes and drained well

salt and pepper

Poaching stock

600 ml (1 pint) chicken stock, preferably home-made (see page 23)

5 cm (2 in) piece lemongrass, split open

1 small fresh red chilli, split open and seeded

4 fresh or dried lime leaves, lightly crushed

2.5 cm (1 in) piece fresh root ginger, sliced

a few fresh coriander stalks

2 tbsp fish sauce

Dipping sauce

1 small fresh red chilli, seeded and finely chopped

1 tsp finely chopped fresh root ginger

2 tbsp lime juice

4 tbsp fish sauce

1 tsp caster sugar

To serve

16 lettuce leaves, all about the same size

25 g (scant 1 oz) fresh coriander leaves

25 g (scant 1 oz) fresh mint leaves

Preparation time: 20 minutes
Cooking time: 20 minutes

1 To make the pigeon rolls, put all the ingredients into a food processor and blend until they are finely chopped, but not puréed, and start to bind together. Turn the mixture out onto a work surface and shape into a roll. Divide into 16 equal portions. Form each into a small rugby-ball shape. Set the pigeon rolls aside on a plate.

2 Put all the ingredients for the poaching stock in a medium-sized pan. Bring to the boil, then simmer for 5 minutes. Spoon in 8 of the pigeon rolls and simmer for 6–7 minutes, turning them every so often with a spoon. Remove them with a draining spoon and put them in a serving dish. Keep warm. Add the rest of the pigeon rolls to the pan and simmer as before.

3 Meanwhile, mix together all the sauce ingredients in a small bowl. Arrange the lettuce leaves on a platter. Put some of the coriander and mint leaves inside each lettuce leaf; garnish the platter with the remaining herbs. Serve the platter of leaves and the bowl of sauce with the warm pigeon rolls.

4 To eat the parcels, take a lettuce leaf, fit a pigeon roll inside and roll up, then dip the parcel into the sauce and enjoy. Alternatively, the sauce can be spooned over the pigeon roll before rolling up, if preferred.

Plus points

- Pigeon offers first-class protein with only a moderate fat content. It is an excellent source of iron and a useful source of zinc. Zinc is vital for normal growth, reproduction and immunity. Pigeon also offers good quantities of vitamin B_6, which helps to release energy from proteins.
- Each portion of this dish provides over 100% of the recommended daily intake of iron for men. Women have a slightly higher iron requirement than men, but this dish still provides 75% of it.
- Rice noodles are gluten-free and wheat-free, making them useful for people with gluten or wheat allergies or intolerance.

Each serving provides

kcal 170, **protein** 18 g, **fat** 8 g (of which saturated fat 1 g), **carbohydrate** 9 g (of which sugars 2 g), **fibre** 0.5 g

✓✓✓	iron
✓✓	B_6
✓	A, copper, zinc

Some more ideas

• Spice up the pigeon mixture with 1 fresh red chilli, seeded, if you like. Chillies are an important flavouring in Vietnamese and Thai cooking. Used raw, chillies are an excellent source of vitamin C, although you'd need to eat a lot to gain much benefit.

• If you can't get fresh shiitake mushrooms, use 15 g (½ oz) dried shiitake mushrooms, rehydrated following the instructions on the packet. Or substitute fresh chestnut or button mushrooms.

• Instead of the pigeon, use 170 g (6 oz) skinless boneless chicken breast and 85 g

(3 oz) cooked tiger prawns or crabmeat. Add 1 tbsp each finely chopped lemongrass (the tender, inner part) and fresh root ginger to the rolls for extra flavour.

• If you don't have fish sauce, soy sauce would do. The thinly pared zest of 1 lime can replace the lime leaves.

Chicken and vegetable filo rolls

These filo pastry rolls make an excellent starter, or you could serve two rolls each for a light meal. The filling is a colourful mixture of low-fat minced chicken and plenty of vegetables, with a little smoked ham and fresh herbs to add to the flavour. The rolls are served with a piquant cranberry relish.

Serves 8 (makes 8)

1 large carrot, about 100 g (3½ oz), cut into very fine matchsticks

75 g (2½ oz) savoy cabbage, finely shredded

2 spring onions, cut into fine shreds

225 g (8 oz) minced chicken

55 g (2 oz) lean smoked ham, finely chopped

½ small onion, finely chopped

2 tbsp fresh white breadcrumbs

2 tsp chopped fresh sage

2 tsp chopped fresh thyme

4 large sheets filo pastry, each about 46 x 28 cm (18 x 11 in)

2 tbsp extra virgin olive oil

15 g (½ oz) butter, melted

1 tsp sesame seeds

salt and pepper

Cranberry relish

3 tbsp cranberry sauce

1 tbsp extra virgin olive oil

1 tbsp red wine vinegar

1 tsp made English mustard

To serve

115 g (4 oz) mixed salad leaves

Preparation time: 40 minutes
Cooking time: 30 minutes

1 Blanch the carrot, cabbage and spring onions in boiling water for 1 minute. Drain, then plunge into a bowl of cold water to refresh. Drain again and pat dry with kitchen paper. Put the vegetables in a large mixing bowl with the chicken, ham, onion, breadcrumbs, herbs and seasoning. Mix together well, then set aside.

2 Preheat the oven to 190°C (375°F, gas mark 5). Halve each filo pastry sheet lengthways and then trim to a strip measuring 36 x 12 cm (15 x 5 in). Mix the oil and butter together.

3 Brush one pastry strip lightly with the butter mixture. Place an eighth of the filling at one end, shaping it into a sausage. Roll up the filling inside the pastry, folding in the long sides as you go, to make a spring roll-shaped parcel. Place on a baking sheet and brush with a little of the butter and oil mixture. Repeat to make another 7 parcels.

4 Score 3 diagonal slashes on top of each parcel. Sprinkle over the sesame seeds. Bake for 30 minutes or until the pastry is golden.

5 Meanwhile, put all the relish ingredients in a screw-top jar, season to taste and shake well.

6 Arrange the mixed salad leaves on serving plates, place a filo roll on each and drizzle around the relish.

Plus points

• Unlike most other types of pastry, filo contains very little fat – in 100 g (3½ oz) filo there are 2 g fat and 300 kcal. The same weight of shortcrust pastry contains 29 g fat and 449 kcal.

• Using a mixture of oil and butter to brush the sheets of filo reduces the amount of saturated fat, and brushing it on sparingly keeps the overall fat content down.

• By bulking out the poultry with plenty of vegetables you reduce the amount of fat in the dish as well as providing extra vitamins and dietary fibre.

Each roll provides

kcal 130, **protein** 8.5 g, **fat** 7.5 g (of which saturated fat 2 g), **carbohydrate** 7 g (of which sugars 4 g), **fibre** 1 g

✓　A, B$_6$

poultry first

48

Some more ideas

• Use minced turkey instead of chicken.

• For Greek-style chicken parcels, cook 30 g
(1 oz) long-grain rice in boiling water for
12 minutes or until just tender; drain and rinse
with cold water. Meanwhile, soften 1 finely
chopped onion in 1 tsp extra virgin olive oil for
5 minutes, then set aside to cool. Put the rice
and onion in a bowl with 225 g (8 oz) minced

chicken or turkey, 2 tbsp toasted pine nuts,
2 tbsp raisins, 2 tbsp chopped fresh mint and
2 tbsp chopped fresh dill. Season to taste. Mix
together well and divide into 8 equal portions.
Cut the sheets of filo pastry into 8 strips as
before. Brush each pastry strip lightly with the
olive oil and butter mixture, and put one portion
of the filling at one end. Fold the pastry over the
filling into a triangle. Continue folding down the

pastry strip to make a triangular-shaped parcel.
Brush all the parcels with the butter and oil
mixture, and scatter over 1 tsp poppy seeds.
Bake for 30 minutes. Serve the filo triangles on
a tomato and onion salad: thickly slice 3 beef
tomatoes and scatter over 1 sliced red onion,
15 small black olives and 1 tbsp chopped fresh
dill. Season with salt and pepper and drizzle
over 1 tbsp extra virgin olive oil.

For Maximum Vitality

Nutritious salads full of colour and crunch

Poultry and game combine well with fresh vegetables and fruit, pasta, rice or bulghur wheat, fresh herbs and aromatic seasonings to make protein-packed salads. Try tender strips of chicken baked in an unusual coating of sesame seeds and cornflakes, and served on crunchy cabbage. Stir-fry chicken with turkey rashers, then toss with avocado and watercress in a sweet-and-sour dressing. Marinate tender quail in Madeira, then grill and serve atop mushrooms and fennel, or make a special Christmas salad of turkey and pecans in a cranberry dressing.

Warm sesame chicken salad

Strips of chicken in a crisp coating of sesame seeds, breadcrumbs and cornflakes are served atop a crunchy vegetable salad dressed with a fresh herb vinaigrette. A little chilli powder in the coating gives a bit of a kick.

Serves 4
450 g (1 lb) skinless boneless chicken
   breasts (fillets)
75 g (2½ oz) fresh white breadcrumbs
50 g (1¾ oz) cornflakes, lightly crushed
4 tsp sesame seeds, plus extra to garnish
1 tsp hot chilli powder, or to taste
2 eggs
salt and pepper
Salad
¼ white cabbage
½ frisée (curly endive)
2 heads chicory
Herb dressing
1 tbsp chopped parsley
1 tbsp chopped fresh oregano
1 tbsp chopped fresh tarragon
1 tbsp white wine vinegar
4 tbsp olive oil
1 tsp clear honey

Preparation time: 15 minutes
Cooking time: 15–20 minutes

Each serving provides
kcal 440, **protein** 32 g, **fat** 23 g (of which saturated fat 5 g), **carbohydrate** 29 g (of which sugars 5 g), **fibre** 2.5 g

✓✓✓	B$_6$, C
✓✓	B$_1$, B$_2$, B$_{12}$, folate, niacin, copper, iron, zinc
✓	A, E, calcium, potassium, selenium

1 Preheat the oven to 200°C (400°F, gas mark 6). Slice each chicken breast in half horizontally, then cut lengthways into strips.

2 Put the breadcrumbs, cornflakes, sesame seeds and chilli powder in a polythene bag and shake to mix well. Break the eggs into a shallow dish and beat together lightly.

3 Dip the chicken strips, one at a time, in the egg, then drop into the polythene bag. When a few pieces of chicken are in the bag, shake to coat evenly with the sesame seed mixture. As the chicken strips are coated, transfer to 2 non-stick baking trays, spreading out the pieces.

4 Bake the chicken strips for 15–20 minutes, turning the pieces over halfway through the baking time.

5 Meanwhile, make the salad. Finely shred the cabbage and place in a large mixing bowl. Pull the frisée and chicory leaves apart and tear any large ones into smaller pieces. Add to the mixing bowl.

6 In a small screw-top jar, shake together the dressing ingredients. Season to taste. Pour the dressing over the salad and toss well.

7 Divide the salad among 4 plates and pile the cooked chicken pieces on top. Garnish with a few more sesame seeds, then serve.

Some more ideas
● Use 125 g (4½ oz) breadcrumbs – white or wholemeal – instead of the mixture of breadcrumbs and cornflakes. Wholemeal crumbs will provide more B vitamins and fibre than white breadcrumbs.

● For a Chinese-style chicken salad, use 1 egg and beat it with 2 tsp five-spice powder, 1 tbsp poppy seeds, 2 tbsp tomato purée, 2 tbsp sweet sherry and 2 tbsp dark soy sauce in a bowl. Stir in the chicken strips. Lift them out, a few at a time, and coat with the breadcrumb mixture (omit the sesame seeds and chilli powder). Bake as above. Meanwhile, finely shred 1 head Chinese leaves, discarding some of the hard white core. Place in a bowl and add 115 g (4 oz) bean sprouts and 1 bunch of spring onions, thinly sliced into rings. Toss with the dressing (made with 1½ tbsp each parsley and fresh coriander). Serve the hot chicken strips on top of the salad.

Plus points
● Cabbage belongs to a family of vegetables which contain a number of different phytochemicals that may help to protect against breast cancer. They are also good sources of vitamin C and among the richest vegetable sources of folate.

● Sesame seeds can provide useful amounts of calcium.

for maximum vitality

52

Stir-fried chicken and avocado salad with hot balsamic dressing

This is an excellent main dish salad, combining stir-fried strips of chicken and smoked turkey rashers in a hot piquant dressing with creamy avocado and sweet cherry tomatoes. Smoked turkey rashers are a great low-fat alternative to bacon, giving a similar savoury flavour.

Serves 4

3 tbsp extra virgin olive oil

2 garlic cloves, cut into slivers

300 g (10½ oz) skinless boneless chicken breasts (fillets), cut into strips

2 tbsp clear honey

1 tbsp balsamic vinegar

1 tbsp wholegrain mustard

150 g (5½ oz) smoked turkey rashers, diced

salt and pepper

Tomato and avocado salad

2 Little Gem lettuces, separated into leaves

55 g (2 oz) watercress sprigs

2 ripe avocados

juice of ½ lemon

250 g (9 oz) cherry tomatoes, halved

1 small red onion, thinly sliced

Preparation time: 15 minutes

Cooking time: 10 minutes

Each serving provides

kcal 385, **protein** 29 g, **fat** 24 g (of which saturated fat 4.5 g), **carbohydrate** 14 g (of which sugars 13 g), **fibre** 4 g

✓✓✓	B_6
✓✓	C, E, niacin, potassium
✓	A, B_1, B_2, B_{12}, folate, copper, iron, selenium, zinc

1 First prepare the salad. Put the lettuce and watercress in a large wide salad bowl. Peel and thickly slice the avocados and toss with the lemon juice to prevent discoloration. Scatter the avocados, tomatoes and red onion on top of the lettuce and watercress. Set the salad aside.

2 Heat the oil in a large frying pan, add the garlic and stir round the pan for just 30 seconds or so until softened. Toss in the strips of chicken and stir-fry for 2–3 minutes or until they change colour.

3 Add the honey, vinegar and mustard, and stir to mix well. Add the diced turkey rashers and stir-fry for 1 more minute or until they are cooked, but still tender and moist (take care not to overcook or they will be dry). Season to taste.

4 Spoon the chicken mixture over the salad. Toss together, then serve immediately with crusty bread.

Some more ideas

● For a turkey and artichoke salad with a lemon dressing, replace the chicken with 2 small skinless turkey breast steaks, about 300 g (10½ oz) in total, and use 2 lean rashers of smoked back bacon instead of the smoked turkey rashers. Stir-fry the turkey with the bacon and garlic for 5–6 minutes or until lightly golden, then add the grated zest and juice of 1 lemon to the pan with the honey and balsamic vinegar (omit the mustard). Instead of the tomato and avocado salad, serve the turkey stir-fry spooned over an artichoke salad made with 100 g (3½ oz) baby spinach leaves, 55 g (2 oz) rocket and a 285 g jar of well-drained antipasto artichokes.

● For a milder flavour, 2 shallots can be used instead of the small red onion.

Plus points

● Turkey rashers, which are widely available in large supermarkets, contain a fraction of the fat of bacon and are lower in calories: 100 g (3½ oz) contains just 1.6 g fat and 99 kcal, compared with 21 g fat and 249 kcal in the same weight of back bacon.

● Avocado is a rich source of monounsaturated fat and of vitamin B_6 – one avocado provides half the recommended daily intake of this vitamin.

for maximum vitality

Pasta and chicken salad with basil

Tempt your family with this healthy and filling pasta salad. Quick to prepare, it makes an ideal midweek supper and won't spoil if someone is late home. Tossing the pasta with lemon juice and white wine not only adds flavour but also means that the quantity of oil can be reduced, so saving on fat.

Serves 4

300 g (10½ oz) pasta quills or shells

100 g (3½ oz) mange-touts

3 tbsp extra virgin olive oil

finely shredded zest and juice of 1 lemon

4 tbsp dry white wine

400 g (14 oz) skinless boneless chicken breasts (fillets), cut into bite-sized chunks

2 garlic cloves, thinly sliced

200 g (7 oz) baby plum tomatoes, halved, or 3 plum tomatoes, each cut into 6 wedges

50 g (1¾ oz) stoned black olives

1 small bunch of fresh basil, about 20 g (¾ oz)

salt and pepper

Preparation time: 15 minutes
Cooking time: 15 minutes

1 Drop the pasta into a large saucepan of boiling water. When the water returns to the boil, cook for 10–12 minutes, or according to the packet instructions, until al dente. Add the mange-touts for the final minute of cooking. Drain, rinse with cold water and drain again well.

2 Mix 2 tbsp of the oil with the lemon zest and juice and the wine in a large salad bowl. Season to taste. Add the pasta and mange-touts, and toss to coat with the dressing. Set aside to cool slightly.

3 Meanwhile, heat the remaining 1 tbsp of oil in a large frying pan. Add the chicken and garlic, and stir-fry over a high heat for 5–6 minutes or until the chicken is lightly browned and thoroughly cooked. Add to the pasta.

4 Scatter the tomatoes and olives over the top. Sprinkle with the basil leaves, tearing larger ones into pieces. Toss the salad together and serve while the chicken is still warm.

Plus points

- The vitamin C provided by the freshly squeezed lemon juice and the tomatoes will aid the absorption of iron from the chicken.
- Pasta is an excellent source of starchy carbohydrate and it is low in fat. It also contains valuable vitamins, in particular the water-soluble B vitamins that we need to take in regularly.

Some more ideas

- For a chicken and couscous salad, use 200 g (7 oz) couscous instead of the pasta. Pour 600 ml (1 pint) boiling water over the couscous and leave to soak for 5 minutes. Drain, then toss with the lemon zest and juice, oil and some seasoning (omit the wine). Stir-fry the strips of chicken, adding 250 g (9 oz) sliced courgettes for the last 2 minutes of cooking. Add to the couscous, together with the tomatoes and olives, and flat-leaf parsley instead of basil. Toss well and serve.
- Use leftover cooked chicken. Mix the cooked chicken with the pasta and mange-touts, and omit step 3. Either leave out the garlic or add 1 crushed garlic clove to the dressing in step 2.

Each serving provides

kcal 470, **protein** 34 g, **fat** 12 g (of which saturated fat 2 g), **carbohydrate** 60 g (of which sugars 4 g), **fibre** 4 g

✓✓	B_1, B_6, C, niacin, copper, iron, selenium
✓	A, B_2, E, folate, potassium, zinc

for maximum vitality

57

Grilled quail salad with Madeira

Here, Madeira and juniper berries add wonderful flavour to a marinade for spatchcocked quail, which is then grilled. Served on a mound of lightly dressed raw vegetables, including fennel, mushrooms and bean sprouts, the quail make a filling main course salad, with bread or rolls to accompany.

Serves 4

8 quail

250 g (9 oz) bulb fennel, trimmed and very finely chopped

200 g (7 oz) mushrooms, such as shiitake or chestnut, thinly sliced

200 g (7 oz) bean sprouts

2 tbsp fresh thyme leaves

mixed salad leaves

Madeira marinade

175 ml (6 fl oz) Madeira

1 tbsp extra virgin olive oil

1 large garlic clove, crushed

1 large sprig of fresh thyme

1 large bay leaf

4 juniper berries, lightly crushed

Vinaigrette dressing

4 tbsp walnut oil or extra virgin olive oil

1½ tbsp white wine vinegar

½ tsp Dijon mustard

pinch of caster sugar

salt and pepper

To garnish

2 spring onions, chopped

sprigs of fresh thyme

Preparation time: about 30 minutes, plus at least 4 hours marinating

Cooking time: 10–12 minutes

1 To spatchcock the birds, use poultry shears or a knife to cut up one side of the backbone, then cut out the backbone altogether. Open out each bird, skin side up, on the chopping board and press down firmly with the palm of your hand to flatten. Carefully remove the skin from each bird.

2 Place all the marinade ingredients in a glass dish or bowl large enough to hold the quail in a single layer. Add the quail and turn them over so they are well coated. Leave them breast side down. Cover and marinate at cool room temperature for 4 hours, or up to 12 hours in the refrigerator.

3 To make the dressing, place all the ingredients in a small screw-top jar and shake until well blended. Set aside.

4 Preheat the grill to high. Lift the quail out of the marinade. Weave 2 parallel skewers through each bird to hold it flat. (If you are using long skewers, thread 2 birds on each pair of skewers.)

5 Place the birds on the grill rack, 15 cm (6 in) from the heat, and grill for 10–12 minutes, basting frequently with the remaining marinade and turning once. To test if the quail are cooked, cut a small slit in the meaty part of the thigh – if the juices run clear, the quail are done.

6 Meanwhile, combine the fennel, mushrooms, bean sprouts and thyme in a mixing bowl. Shake the dressing, then pour over the vegetables and toss until well coated. Divide the mixed salad leaves among 4 plates and top with the dressed vegetables.

7 Remove the skewers from the quail. Place 2 quail on each bed of vegetables, garnish with spring onions and thyme sprigs, and serve.

Plus points

- Like other game birds, quail are low in fat.
- Traditional game marinades include a lot of oil, but this recipe uses a full-flavoured fortified wine to add flavour and only the minimum of extra virgin olive oil to keep the quail moist during grilling.
- Bean sprouts are a good source of vitamin C, and also contain small amounts of the B-group vitamins as well as potassium and iron. The mushrooms contain vitamin B_2, and they are a good source of copper.
- By serving the vegetables raw in a salad you preserve many of the vitamins that would be destroyed by cooking. For maximum benefit, prepare the vegetables just before serving.

Some more ideas

● Substitute 675 g (1 ½ lb) skinned chicken thighs or breasts on the bone; you will not need to skewer them. For the marinade, replace the Madeira with a full-bodied red wine, such as a Burgundy. Grill the chicken for 12–15 minutes, turning the pieces several times and basting with the marinade, until the juices run clear when the meat is pierced with a knife. Slice the meat off the bones and arrange on top of the salad for serving.

● Another high-fibre salad that is delicious with the quail or chicken pieces can be made with 1 sweet onion, such as Vidalia, finely chopped, 250 g (9 oz) grated courgette, 250 g (9 oz) grated carrot and 4 tbsp finely chopped parsley. Use the same dressing, made with extra virgin olive oil. Serve on radicchio leaves or spinach leaves for a contrast in colour. If you want to bulk out the salad, stir in a handful of blanched fresh sweetcorn kernels (or frozen sweetcorn thawed with boiling water).

Each serving provides

kcal 300, **protein** 19 g, **fat** 19 g (of which saturated fat 1.5 g), **carbohydrate** 5.5 g (of which sugars 4.5 g), **fibre** 3 g

✓✓✓	B_{12}, copper, iron
✓✓	B_2, B_6, folate
✓	B_1, C, niacin, potassium, zinc

Smoked chicken and fruit salad

With tender smoked chicken, mixed rice and refreshing melon and pineapple, this salad is as satisfying as it is delicious. It doesn't have an oil-based dressing to pile on the calories – just freshly squeezed orange juice and the juices from the other fruits. This salad is best eaten on the day it is made.

Serves 4

340 g (12 oz) mixed long-grain rice and wild rice

300 g (10½ oz) skinned and boned smoked chicken breast, cut into bite-sized pieces

250 g (9 oz) melon flesh, such as Galia, some scooped into balls and the rest cut into bite-sized pieces

250 g (9 oz) pineapple flesh, cut into bite-sized pieces

finely grated zest and juice of 1 large orange

salt and pepper

To serve

Cos lettuce leaves

4 tbsp finely chopped fresh tarragon or parsley

Preparation time: about 45 minutes, plus cooling

1 Put the long-grain and wild rice in a saucepan and add water to cover by a depth of 4 cm (1½ in). Bring to the boil, then reduce the heat and simmer, uncovered, for about 15 minutes or until tender (or according to the packet instructions). Drain well in a colander and set aside to cool.

2 Tip the cooled rice into a large bowl. Add the chicken, melon and pineapple, and fold together gently.

3 Stir in the orange zest and 3 tbsp orange juice, adding more if liked. Season to taste.

4 Line a serving bowl with the lettuce leaves. Spoon in the salad, sprinkle with the chopped herbs and serve, or cover and chill until required.

Plus points

- Rice is an ideal ingredient to include in a healthy diet because it is a complex carbohydrate and it is low in fat.
- Squeeze the orange juice just before you add it to the salad, to preserve the vitamin C. The vitamin C will aid the absorption of iron from the chicken.
- This salad is rich in vitamins – B vitamins in the rice and vitamin C in the melon and pineapple. The fruits also provide fibre.

Some more ideas

- Boost the fibre content by grating in a carrot, or adding 1 celery stick, finely chopped.
- Replace the rice with Puy lentils, a good source of B vitamins. Cook the lentils according to the instructions on the packet.
- Fresh mint or fennel can replace the tarragon or parsley.
- For variety, try a smoked turkey and red rice salad. Cook 200 g (7 oz) Camargue red rice in boiling water for 30 minutes or until tender (or according to the packet instructions). Drain and leave to cool. Meanwhile, soak 115 g (4 oz) dried cherries in boiling water for 20 minutes; drain well and pat dry. Put the rice and cherries in a large bowl. Add 340 g (12 oz) skinned and boned smoked turkey breast, cut into bite-sized pieces, and 2 Asian pears or ordinary pears, peeled and diced. Sprinkle with the finely grated zest of 1 large orange and toss gently to mix. Finish with 4 tbsp finely chopped fresh tarragon.

Each serving provides

kcal 440, **protein** 21.5 g, **fat** 4 g (of which saturated fat 1 g), **carbohydrate** 83 g (of which sugars 10 g), **fibre** 1.5 g

✓✓✓	B_6
✓✓	C, niacin, copper
✓	B_1, folate, iron, potassium, selenium, zinc

Marinated duck salad with bulghur

The contrast of sweet citrus, slightly bitter greens, spicy chilli, earthy grains and tender duck is marvellous, with sweet basil adding an unexpected note. Kumquats are a curious citrus fruit in that they are eaten skin and all; poaching takes away their bitterness so they yield up a sweet citrus flavour.

Serves 4

150 g (5½ oz) bulghur wheat

4 small boneless duck breasts, about 500 g (1 lb 2 oz) in total

3 garlic cloves, chopped

1½ tbsp mild chilli powder

1½ tsp ground cumin

4 tbsp finely shredded fresh basil

grated zest and juice of 1 orange, plus juice of 2 more oranges

juice of 1½ lemons

2 tbsp extra virgin olive oil

16 kumquats

1½ tbsp sugar

3 spring onions, thinly sliced

3 tbsp chopped fresh coriander

200 g (7 oz) salad leaves

2 tsp balsamic vinegar, or to taste

¼ cucumber, finely diced

½ large (beefsteak) tomato, finely diced

salt and pepper

Preparation time: 45 minutes
Cooking time: 10 minutes

Each serving provides

kcal 440, **protein** 30 g, **fat** 15 g (of which saturated fat 3.5 g), **carbohydrate** 48 g (of which sugars 19 g), **fibre** 4 g

✓✓✓	B₁, B₁₂, C, copper, iron
✓✓	B₂, B₆, folate, niacin, potassium, zinc
✓	A, E, calcium

1 Place the bulghur wheat in a bowl and cover with boiling water. Leave to soak for about 30 minutes.

2 Meanwhile, remove all of the skin and fat from the duck breasts. Put the breasts in a dish and add half of the garlic, chilli powder, cumin and basil, all of the zest and juice of 1 orange, the juice of ½ lemon and ½ tbsp of the olive oil. Mix well, turning the breasts to coat, then set aside to marinate.

3 To prepare the kumquats, cut a small slit in each one (do not cut all the way through). Place the kumquats in a saucepan with the juice of 1 orange, the sugar and 175 ml (6 fl oz) of water. Bring to the boil and simmer over a moderate heat, turning the kumquats so that they cook evenly, for 15–20 minutes or until they are just tender and the liquid has reduced by about half. Remove from the heat and leave to cool in the liquid.

4 Drain the soaked bulghur wheat and return it to the bowl. Add the spring onions, the remaining garlic, chilli powder, cumin, lemon juice and orange juice, 1 tbsp of the remaining olive oil and the coriander. Season to taste.

5 Heat a ridged cast-iron grill pan or non-stick frying pan. Remove the duck from its marinade and brown on both sides over a high heat. Cook for a further 4–5 minutes, turning the breasts frequently so that they don't stick or burn. The meat will be rosy in colour in the centre (cook a little longer if you prefer it well done). Remove the breasts to a carving board and slice very thinly against the grain.

6 Arrange the salad leaves and remaining basil on 4 plates and place 4 kumquats on each bed of leaves. Drizzle with the remaining ½ tbsp olive oil, the balsamic vinegar and a little of the kumquat cooking liquid. Place a portion of the bulghur wheat salad in the centre of each plate, and arrange the duck slices around it. Scatter on the diced cucumber and tomato, and serve immediately.

Plus points

• Oranges and kumquats are both an excellent source of vitamin C. They also contain compounds called coumarins which are believed to help thin the blood, thus helping to prevent stroke and heart attacks.

• Bulghur wheat is a good, low-fat source of starchy (complex) carbohydrate. It contains useful amounts of some of the B vitamins, particularly B₁, as well as copper and iron.

for maximum vitality

Some more ideas

• Instead of bulghur wheat, use quinoa, a nutty little grain that comes from Peru. Rinse 75 g (2½ oz) quinoa grains well (they are coated with a sticky substance), then place in a saucepan and add 125 ml (4½ fl oz) of boiling water, or vegetable cooking water such as that from cooking corn on the cob. Bring to the boil, then cover and simmer for about 10 minutes or until the grains are just tender and have absorbed the liquid. Fluff up with a fork and then dress as for the bulghur wheat.

• Add a North African flavour to the marinade for the duck breasts. In addition to the spices above, add ¼ tsp each of ground ginger, cinnamon and coriander and ¼ tsp mild or medium curry powder. Double the amount of lemon juice.

Turkey salad with red cabbage

This is a lovely crunchy salad for winter, full of contrasting tastes and tossed with an unusual dressing made from cranberry sauce and walnut oil. Red cabbage makes an interesting base, but does tend to stain the other ingredients, so serve the salad as soon as everything has been mixed together.

Serves 4

55 g (2 oz) pecan nuts, coarsely chopped
½ tsp caraway seeds
300 g (10½ oz) cold roast turkey meat,
   without skin, diced
200 g (7 oz) red cabbage, finely shredded
3 celery sticks, sliced
2 carrots, grated
30 g (1 oz) sultanas or raisins

Cranberry dressing

2 tbsp cranberry sauce
2 tbsp extra virgin olive oil
2 tbsp walnut oil
2 tbsp red wine vinegar
salt and pepper

Preparation time: about 20 minutes

1 Put all the ingredients for the dressing into a salad bowl and whisk together until well blended and starting to emulsify.

2 Place the pecan nuts and caraway seeds in a small, dry frying pan and toast over a low heat, stirring occasionally, for 3–5 minutes or until the pecans are golden and you can smell the nutty fragrance. Tip into a clean bowl and leave to cool slightly.

3 Put the turkey, red cabbage, celery and carrots into the bowl with the dressing. Add the toasted pecan nuts and caraway seeds and the sultanas or raisins, and mix until all the ingredients are well coated with the dressing. Serve immediately.

Some more ideas

● Use white cabbage instead of red, and substitute green or red-skinned dessert apples for the carrots and sultanas.

● For a summer salad, make the dressing with 4 tbsp extra virgin olive oil, 2 tsp Dijon mustard, 1 tbsp clear honey, 2 tbsp lemon juice, 2 tsp finely grated fresh root ginger and seasoning to taste. Stir the diced turkey into the dressing. Steam 250 g (9 oz) asparagus, cut into bite-sized pieces, with 100 g (3½ oz) shelled fresh broad beans, 200 g (7 oz) small sugarsnap peas and 400 g (14 oz) sliced new potatoes for 10 minutes or until just tender. (If the skins of the broad beans are a little tough, peel them away to reveal the bright green and tender bean beneath.) Toss the vegetables with the turkey and dressing while still hot. Fold in 2 tbsp snipped fresh chives. Serve warm or at room temperature.

Plus points

● Pecan nuts are a rich source of essential fatty acids and polyunsaturated fats.
● Cranberries contain a compound that helps to prevent *E. coli* bacteria from causing urinary tract infections.
● Red cabbage provides useful amounts of the B vitamin folate, vitamin C and potassium. Potassium helps to protect against the adverse effects of a high salt intake on blood pressure.

Each serving provides

kcal 340, **protein** 25 g, **fat** 22 g (of which saturated fat 2.5 g), **carbohydrate** 12 g (of which sugars 11 g), **fibre** 3 g

✓✓✓	C
✓✓	B_6, B_{12}, niacin, copper
✓	A, B_1, E, folate, iron, potassium, zinc

for maximum vitality

65

Creamy chicken salad with ginger

This creamy yet light chicken salad is ideal for serving as a luncheon or cold buffet dish. Basing the dressing on soured cream mixed with mayonnaise makes it lower in fat than many other creamy dressings while still keeping the richness. Don't be tempted to omit the stem ginger – its subtle flavour makes all the difference.

Serves 6

1 cold roasted chicken, about 1.5 kg (3 lb 3 oz), or 675 g (1½ lb) cooked chicken meat

1 tbsp lime juice

2 crisp, green-skinned dessert apples such as Granny Smith

4 celery sticks, thinly sliced

115 g (4 oz) ready-to-eat dried apricots, quartered

5 tbsp soured cream

2 tbsp mayonnaise

2 pieces stem ginger, finely diced

30 g (1 oz) broken walnuts

pepper

sprigs of watercress to garnish

Preparation time: 20–25 minutes

1 If using a whole roast chicken, remove the meat from the carcass, discarding the skin. Cut the chicken meat into bite-sized pieces and place in a large serving bowl.

2 Put the lime juice in a small bowl. Core and chop the apples, then add them to the lime juice and toss well to coat the apple pieces (this will prevent them from turning brown). Add the apples, celery and apricots to the chicken and mix together.

3 Combine the soured cream and mayonnaise in another small bowl and season with pepper. Stir in the stem ginger. Spoon this dressing over the chicken salad and toss until all the pieces are coated. Sprinkle over the walnuts and serve garnished with watercress.

Some more ideas

- Serve this at Christmas time, using leftover turkey instead of chicken.
- Substitute ready-to-eat dried pears for the dried apricots.
- Add 85 g (3 oz) seedless green grapes, halved, or 2 slices of fresh pineapple, cut into small wedges.
- Use toasted hazelnuts or pecan nuts instead of the walnuts.
- Serve the salad on a bed of baby spinach leaves or a mixture of spinach and watercress. Or use your favourite salad leaves.
- Use reduced-calorie mayonnaise to cut the fat even further.

Plus points

- This recipe offers useful amounts of dietary fibre, from the dried apricots, apples with their skins and celery. Fibre is essential to keep the digestive tract healthy.
- Dried apricots provide useful quantities of vitamin A (from beta-carotene), and are one of the richest fruit sources of iron.
- Some studies indicate that eating a small quantity of walnuts daily, as part of a low-fat diet, can help to reduce high blood cholesterol levels. Walnuts also provide useful amounts of vitamin E, some of the B vitamins, potassium and protein.

Each serving provides

kcal 350, **protein** 36 g, **fat** 18 g (of which saturated fat 4 g), **carbohydrate** 11 g (of which sugars 11 g), **fibre** 2 g

✓✓✓	B_6, niacin
✓✓	E, copper
✓	A, B_2, iron, potassium, selenium, zinc

for maximum vitality

Japanese chicken salad

The ingredients for this salad are presented individually on a platter rather than being mixed together, with a simple tahini-based dressing so everyone can help themselves. Typical of Japanese cooking, there is a fairly small amount of meat per person, but plenty of raw vegetables to crunch through and fill you up.

Serves 4

2 skinless boneless chicken breasts (fillets), about 300 g (10½ oz) in total
1 tbsp mirin or sake
salt and pepper

Tahini dressing
2 tbsp tahini
1 small garlic clove, crushed (optional)
1 tbsp soy sauce
2 tsp lemon juice, or to taste
chilli powder to garnish

Salad
10 cm (4 in) piece cucumber
2 carrots
1 red pepper, seeded
2 Little Gem lettuces, separated into leaves
handful of fresh basil leaves, finely shredded
handful of fresh mint leaves, finely shredded
8 spring onions, halved lengthways
115 g (4 oz) button mushrooms, thinly sliced

Preparation time: 25–30 minutes, plus cooling

Each serving provides

kcal 170, protein 20 g, fat 7.5 g (of which saturated fat 1.5 g), **carbohydrate** 6 g (of which sugars 5.5 g), fibre 3 g

✓✓✓	A, B₆, C
✓✓	folate, niacin, copper, iron
✓	B₁, B₂, potassium, selenium, zinc

1 Place the chicken breasts on a heatproof plate in a steamer set over gently boiling water. Sprinkle with the mirin or sake and a little seasoning. Cover and steam for 10–12 minutes or until cooked. Set aside to cool.

2 To make the dressing, mix all the ingredients, except the chilli powder, in a bowl. Drain the cooking juices from the chicken and make up to 4 tbsp with water. Add to the dressing. Taste and add more lemon juice, if necessary. Pour into a serving bowl and sprinkle with a pinch of chilli powder.

3 For the salad, cut the cucumber, carrots and red pepper into fine strips of similar length, about 5 cm (2 in). Arrange the lettuce leaves at one end of a large platter. Scatter over the shredded basil and mint. Cut the chicken into strips and place on the lettuce. Arrange all the other salad ingredients attractively on the platter. Serve with the dressing in a separate bowl for people to help themselves.

Some more ideas

● Make a Chinese-style salad by halving the amount of carrot, cucumber and red pepper and adding instead ½ can of bamboo shoots, well drained, about 12 canned water chestnuts, thinly sliced, 125 g (4½ oz) fresh bean sprouts, and a few baby sweetcorn, cooked and sliced lengthways. Instead of arranging the salad on a platter, mix the ingredients and pile them high in a large bowl or individual bowls. Make a dressing from 4 tbsp bottled plum sauce, 2 tbsp soy sauce, 2 tbsp toasted sesame oil and 1–2 tsp lemon juice with a pinch of caster sugar. Sprinkle a few toasted sesame seeds on top of each salad.

● If you don't have tahini, toast 4 tbsp sesame seeds in a dry frying pan and then pound them in a pestle and mortar, adding a tiny bit of sesame or sunflower oil to make a paste.

● For a vegetarian salad, use 250 g (9 oz) marinated or smoked tofu, sliced or diced, instead of the steamed chicken.

Plus points

● Because all the vegetables are eaten raw, this salad offers excellent amounts of vitamin C, which will aid the absorption of iron from the chicken. The vegetables are also an excellent source of fibre and of beta-carotene, which with vitamin C plays a role in protecting against cancer.

● Mushrooms provide useful amounts of some of the B vitamins as well as good quantities of the trace mineral copper. Copper is a component of many enzymes and is needed for bone growth and the formation of connective tissues.

for maximum vitality

Quick Poultry Dishes

Sustaining meals in 30 minutes or less

Poultry is particularly succulent when it is cooked quickly, so it is ideal when you're short of time. Enjoy pan-fried turkey escalopes with a piquant pan sauce and French beans. Try strips of duck Chinese-spiced and stir-fried with crunchy greens, bean sprouts and sweet pear. Sauté chicken thighs with artichokes, red peppers and olives. Or grill chicken breasts tandoori-style and serve with a simple raita. Herby polenta makes a starchy base for turkey in a creamy sauce, while potatoes and sweetcorn turn chicken into a satisfying supper.

Spiced stir-fried duck

Here, strips of duck are stir-fried in the Chinese fashion, with onions, water chestnuts, pak choy, bean sprouts and – a sweet touch – fresh pear. Very little oil is needed for a stir-fry, and adding lots of vegetables keeps the quantity of meat down. Serve with rice noodles or with plain boiled or steamed rice.

Serves 4

400 g (14 oz) boneless duck breasts

2 tsp five-spice powder

2 tbsp sunflower oil

100 g (3½ oz) button onions, thinly sliced

4 small celery sticks, thinly sliced, plus a few leaves to garnish

1 large firm pear, peeled, cored and diced

1 can water chestnuts, about 225 g, drained and sliced

1 tbsp clear honey

3 tbsp rice vinegar or sherry vinegar

1 tbsp light soy sauce

200 g (7 oz) pak choy, shredded

150 g (5½ oz) bean sprouts

Preparation time: about 15 minutes

Cooking time: about 10 minutes

Each serving provides

kcal 200, protein 13 g, fat 9 g (of which saturated fat 2 g), carbohydrate 17 g (of which sugars 13 g), fibre 2.5 g

✓✓✓	B₁₂
✓✓	B₆, C, E, folate, copper, iron
✓	B₁, B₂, niacin, calcium, potassium, zinc

1 Remove the skin and all fat from the duck breasts, then cut them across into thin strips. Sprinkle with the five-spice powder and toss to coat. Set aside for a few minutes while the vegetables are prepared.

2 Heat a wok or heavy-based frying pan until really hot, then add the oil and swirl to coat the wok. Add the duck pieces and stir-fry for 2 minutes. Add the onions and celery and continue to stir-fry for 3 minutes or until softened. Add the pear and water chestnuts and stir to mix.

3 Add the honey, rice vinegar and soy sauce. When the liquid is bubbling, reduce the heat to low and simmer for 2 minutes.

4 Turn the heat up to high again. Add the pak choy and bean sprouts, and stir-fry for 1 minute or until the pak choy is just wilted and the bean sprouts are heated through.

5 Transfer to a warmed serving dish and serve immediately, garnished with celery leaves.

Plus points

- Removing the skin and fat from duck lowers the fat content substantially. Skinless duck breast contains only a fraction more fat than skinless chicken breast.
- Dark green, leafy vegetables such as pak choy provide good amounts of vitamin C, as well as vitamin B₆, folate and niacin.
- Bean sprouts are a good source of vitamin C and also offer B vitamins.
- Water chestnuts provide small amounts of potassium, iron and fibre, but their big advantage is that they contain no fat and very few calories.

Some more ideas

- For a less piquant sauce, replace the rice vinegar or sherry vinegar with red wine or apple or orange juice.
- If in season, use an Asian pear instead of an ordinary pear. Or substitute 3–4 ripe but firm plums, sliced, for the pear.
- For a duck stir-fry with a citrus flavour, use ground star anise instead of five-spice powder, and 170 g (6 oz) sliced and seeded kumquats instead of the pear. Replace the pak choy with ½ head Chinese leaves, shredded. Instead of rice vinegar, use orange juice or red wine.
- Use skinless boneless chicken or turkey breasts, cut into strips, instead of the duck.

quick poultry dishes

Pan-fried turkey escalopes with citrus honey sauce

The tanginess of citrus fruit marries extremely well with poultry, especially turkey which can sometimes be a little light on flavour. Here, orange and lemon, together with honey and shallots, create a tasty sauce for turkey escalopes, served on a stack of green beans. For a simple accompaniment, steam some new potatoes.

Serves 4

4 small skinless turkey breast steaks, about
   115 g (4 oz) each

30 g (1 oz) butter

4 large shallots, thinly sliced

1 garlic clove, crushed

400 g (14 oz) fine French beans, trimmed

2 tbsp clear honey

grated zest and juice of 1 orange

grated zest and juice of 1 lemon

salt and pepper

Preparation time: 15 minutes

Cooking time: about 15 minutes

Each serving provides

kcal 245, **protein** 27 g, **fat** 9 g (of which saturated fat 5 g), **carbohydrate** 14 g (of which sugars 13 g), **fibre** 2.5 g

✓✓✓	B₁₂
✓✓	B₆, C, folate, niacin, iron, zinc
✓	A, copper, potassium

1 Put the turkey steaks between sheets of cling film and pound them to flatten to about 5 mm (¼ in) thickness. Set these escalopes aside.

2 Melt the butter in a large frying pan, add the shallots and garlic, and cook, stirring, for 2–3 minutes or until softened but not brown. Remove the shallots from the pan with a draining spoon and set aside.

3 Put the turkey escalopes in the pan, in one layer, and fry them for 2–3 minutes on each side.

4 Meanwhile, cook the beans in a saucepan of boiling salted water for 3–4 minutes or until just tender. Drain and rinse briefly in cold water to stop the cooking. Keep the beans warm.

5 Mix the honey with the zest and juice of the orange and lemon. Remove the turkey escalopes from the pan and keep hot. Pour the honey mixture into the pan, return the shallots and garlic, and add seasoning to taste. Bring to the boil and bubble for about 2 minutes, stirring constantly.

6 Make a pile of beans on 4 plates and place a turkey escalope on top of each pile. Spoon over the sliced shallots and pan juices, and serve.

Some more ideas

• Use 4 skinless boneless turkey breast fillets, about 125 g (4½ oz) each. Being a bit thicker than escalopes, they will need to be cooked for 5 minutes on each side.

• Replace the turkey steaks with 4 small boneless duck breasts, about 550 g (1¼ lb) in total. Remove the skin and all fat from the breasts. Pan-fry for 3 minutes on each side, if you like duck a little pink, or a little longer for well-done duck. For the sauce, use the zest and juice from a pink grapefruit instead of the orange and lemon. Also add a piece of stem ginger, cut into fine slivers, and 1 tbsp of the stem ginger syrup.

• Replace the beans with 3 finely shredded leeks, stir-fried in 1 tbsp sunflower oil.

Plus points

• Turkey contains even less fat than chicken, making it one of the lowest fat meats available.

• All citrus fruits are an excellent source of vitamin C. Studies have shown a correlation between a regular intake of vitamin C and the maintenance of intellectual function in elderly people.

Chicken and artichoke sauté

Chicken with artichokes is a classic flavour combination, here given a Mediterranean touch with thin slices of red pepper, black olives, thyme and a hint of lemon. Boiled rice or new potatoes are ideal accompaniments for this vitamin-packed dish that is healthily low in calories and saturated fat.

Serves 4

4 tbsp plain flour

1 tbsp dried thyme

8 skinless boneless chicken thighs, about 450 g (1 lb) in total

3 tbsp sunflower oil

1 garlic clove, crushed

1 can artichokes (canned in water), about 400 g, drained and halved

2 red peppers, seeded and thinly sliced

85 g (3 oz) stoned black olives, halved

4 tbsp dry white wine

125 ml (4½ fl oz) chicken stock, preferably home-made (see page 23)

finely grated zest of 1 lemon

salt and pepper

To garnish

sprigs of fresh thyme

lemon wedges

Preparation time: about 5 minutes
Cooking time: 20 minutes

Each serving provides

kcal 350, **protein** 25 g, **fat** 17 g (of which saturated fat 3.5 g), **carbohydrate** 21.5 g (of which sugars 6 g), **fibre** 2.5 g

✓✓✓	A, B$_6$, B$_{12}$, C
✓✓	E, niacin, copper, iron
✓	B$_1$, B$_2$, potassium, selenium, zinc

1 Place the flour and dried thyme in a large polythene bag and season with salt and pepper. Add the chicken thighs to the bag, a few at a time, and shake until they are lightly and evenly coated. Remove the chicken to a plate, shaking off any excess coating. Preheat the oven to its lowest setting.

2 Heat a large, heavy-based frying pan, preferably non-stick, over a high heat. Reduce the heat to moderate and add the oil. When the oil is hot, add the thighs, smooth side down, and sauté for about 3 minutes, moving them around occasionally to prevent them from sticking, until they are golden brown. (If the pan is not large enough to hold the thighs in a single layer, fry them in batches.)

3 Turn the thighs over and cook for a further 8 minutes or until the juices run clear when they are pierced with a knife. Transfer the thighs to a heatproof platter lined with a double thickness of kitchen paper, then place in the oven to keep warm.

4 Pour off excess oil from the pan, leaving just a film, then add the garlic and cook for 10 seconds, stirring. Add the artichokes and red peppers, and sauté for 3–5 minutes, stirring frequently, until the peppers are tender. Stir in the black olives.

5 Add the wine and allow to bubble, stirring, until it has evaporated. Stir in the stock and lemon zest, bring to the boil and cook until reduced by about half. Season to taste.

6 Transfer the chicken thighs to serving plates and spoon the artichoke and pepper mixture alongside. Garnish with thyme sprigs and lemon wedges, and serve.

Plus points

• As well as being low in calories and fat, globe artichokes provide calcium and vitamins A and C.

• Although olives have a high fat content, most of this fat is unsaturated, the type of fat believed to be the most healthy to consume.

• Investing in a good-quality non-stick frying pan makes sense if you want to keep fat consumption low. But whatever pan you use, if you heat it before you add the oil, you will not need as much because the food is less likely to stick to a hot pan.

Some more ideas

● You can prepare 4 skinless turkey breast fillets in the same way.

● For a colourful variation, replace the red peppers with yellow or orange peppers, the olives with 200 g (7 oz) sliced courgettes and the artichokes with 100 g (3½ oz) sliced meaty mushrooms, such as shiitake. Sauté the mushrooms with the garlic until they give off their juices, then add the peppers and courgettes and sauté for 3–5 minutes or until the courgettes are just tender but not too soft.

● Use 225 g (8 oz) asparagus tips, or chopped large asparagus spears, instead of the artichokes. Add with the red peppers.

Polenta with turkey and wild mushroom sauce

This flavoursome dish is a lovely way to enjoy a small amount of leftover turkey or chicken, with lots of tasty mushrooms and a herby soft polenta. The sauce is very quick to make and can be served in many other ways, such as over plain boiled or steamed rice or to stuff baked potatoes.

Serves 4

15 g (½ oz) butter

1 tbsp extra virgin olive oil

115 g (4 oz) shallots or onion, finely chopped

1 garlic clove, crushed (optional)

300 g (10½ oz) chestnut mushrooms, sliced

170 g (6 oz) mixed wild mushrooms, pulled into pieces or sliced

3 tbsp dry sherry

1 tbsp tomato purée

200 g (7 oz) cooked turkey meat, without skin, cut into chunks

4 tbsp single cream

salt and pepper

sprigs of fresh flat-leaf parsley to garnish

Herby polenta

1 litre (1¾ pints) chicken stock, preferably home-made (see page 23), or vegetable stock

200 g (7 oz) instant polenta

3 tbsp finely chopped fresh flat-leaf parsley

Preparation time: 10 minutes
Cooking time: 15 minutes

1 Heat the butter and oil in a large frying pan, add the shallots or onion and garlic, and cook over a moderate heat for 2 minutes or until softened but not brown.

2 Add all the mushrooms to the pan and cook, stirring frequently, for 3–4 minutes or until just softening and the juices are beginning to run.

3 Add the sherry, tomato purée and chunks of turkey, and stir to mix well. Reduce the heat to low and leave to heat through.

4 Meanwhile, prepare the polenta. Bring the stock to the boil in a saucepan, then gradually pour in the polenta, stirring constantly. When all the polenta has been added, stir in the parsley. Reduce the heat to moderate and cook for 2 minutes, stirring, until the polenta is thick. Season to taste.

5 Add the cream to the turkey and mushroom sauce and stir to mix, then remove from the heat. Taste and add seasoning, if required.

6 Spoon the polenta to one side of 4 warmed plates and serve the sauce alongside. Garnish with parsley sprigs.

Some more ideas

● Enrich the sauce with Greek-style yogurt instead of cream.

● Make a simpler, everyday version of the sauce using 450 g (1 lb) button mushrooms. Omit the sherry and flavour instead with 2 tsp Worcestershire sauce. This is particularly good with baked potatoes.

● For a very special flavour, replace the sherry and tomato purée with a few drops of truffle oil or truffle paste. Serve with rice – wild rice or red Carmargue rice are ideal.

Plus points

● Mushrooms are low in fat and calories – 0.5 g fat and 13 kcal in 100 g (3½ oz).

● Polenta is a good gluten-free source of starchy carbohydrate.

Each serving provides

kcal 380, **protein** 23 g, **fat** 12.5 g (of which saturated fat 5 g), **carbohydrate** 41 g (of which sugars 3 g), **fibre** 3 g

✓✓✓	B_{12}, copper
✓✓	B_2, B_6, C, folate, niacin, iron
✓	A, B_1, potassium, selenium, zinc

Indian-style grilled chicken breasts

Tandoori dishes are one of the healthiest options in most Indian restaurants because the food is cooked in a tandoor oven without fat. At home, using a hot grill gives similar results. These lean chicken breasts are served with creamy raita. All that is needed to complete the meal is some boiled rice or naan bread.

Serves 4

4 skinless boneless chicken breasts (fillets),
  about 140 g (5 oz) each
sunflower oil for brushing
lemon or lime wedges to serve
sprigs of fresh coriander to garnish

Yogurt marinade

1 garlic clove, crushed
1 tbsp finely chopped fresh root ginger
1½ tsp tomato purée
1½ tsp garam masala
1½ tsp ground coriander
1½ tsp ground cumin
¼ tsp turmeric
pinch of cayenne pepper, or to taste
100 g (3½ oz) plain low-fat yogurt

Raita

340 g (12 oz) plain low-fat yogurt
1 cucumber, about 300 g (10½ oz), cut into
  quarters lengthways and seeded
100 g (3½ oz) tomato, very finely chopped
½ tsp ground coriander
½ tsp ground cumin
pinch of cayenne pepper
pinch of salt

Preparation time: about 15 minutes
Cooking time: 15 minutes

1 Preheat the grill to high. To make the marinade, put all the marinade ingredients into a large bowl and whisk together well. If you prefer, put the ingredients in a blender or food processor and process until well blended. Transfer to a bowl large enough to hold all the chicken breasts.

2 Score 2 slits on each side of the chicken breasts. Place them in the marinade, turning to coat and rubbing the marinade into the slits. (If you have time, leave the chicken to marinate in the fridge overnight.)

3 Brush the grill rack with oil, then place the chicken breasts on top. Grill for 12–15 minutes, turning and basting with the remaining marinade, until the juices run clear when the chicken is pierced with a knife, and the marinade looks slightly charred.

4 Meanwhile, make the raita. Place the yogurt in a bowl. Coarsely grate the cucumber, then squeeze to remove as much moisture as possible. Add the cucumber to the yogurt together with the tomato, ground coriander, cumin, cayenne and salt. Stir well to mix. Spoon the raita into a serving bowl.

5 Transfer the chicken breasts to a serving plate. Add lemon or lime wedges and garnish with coriander sprigs. Serve with the raita on the side.

Plus points

● Chicken is a low-fat source of protein and this marinade adds very little extra fat.

● Yogurt is an excellent source of protein and calcium, needed for healthy bones and teeth, and it provides useful amounts of phosphorus and vitamins B_2 and B_{12}, as well as beneficial bacteria.

Each serving provides

kcal 250, **protein** 40 g, **fat** 5 g (of which saturated fat 1.5 g), **carbohydrate** 11 g (of which sugars 11 g), **fibre** 1 g

✓✓✓	B_6, niacin
✓✓	B_2, calcium, potassium, selenium
✓	B_1, B_{12}, C, E, folate, copper, iron, zinc

quick poultry dishes

80

Some more ideas

• For a crisper texture on the grilled breasts, omit the yogurt from the marinade, double all the other ingredients and stir in 1 tbsp white distilled vinegar.

• Try this onion and herb raita with either version of the grilled chicken breasts: very finely chop 200 g (7 oz) sweet onion, such as Vidalia, or the same weight of spring onions, and place in a bowl. Stir in 4–6 tbsp finely chopped fresh mint, 2 tbsp finely chopped fresh coriander, 1 fresh green chilli or to taste, finely chopped, and 340 g (12 oz) plain low-fat yogurt. Heat a dry frying pan over a high heat, add 2 tsp cumin seeds and fry, stirring constantly, until they give off their aroma and start to jump. Immediately tip them on top of the raita.

• For Indian-style kebabs, cut the breasts into cubes before you put them in the marinade. While preheating the grill, soak 8 bamboo skewers in water. Thread the chicken cubes onto the skewers, alternating with chunks of courgette and red and yellow pepper cubes. Grill, basting with the marinade and turning the skewers over several times, for 12–15 minutes or until the chicken juices run clear.

• A quick alternative to raita is to serve the chicken breasts with a simple salad of chopped tomatoes and onions on lettuce leaves with finely chopped coriander sprinkled over the top.

Chinese-style omelette

This is a dish you will find wherever Chinese culture flourishes, no matter how far from China's shores. Combining fresh Chinese vegetables with bits of turkey or chicken is a great way to stretch a small amount of protein. Use a non-stick pan or a heavy, well-seasoned frying pan so that you need only a small amount of oil.

Serves 4

100 g (3½ oz) minced turkey

2 tsp soy sauce

2 tbsp sunflower oil

200 g (7 oz) Chinese leaves, cut into shreds

100 g (3½ oz) bean sprouts

30 g (1 oz) frozen peas, thawed with boiling
    water and drained

125 g (4½ oz) smoked turkey or chicken, cut
    into thin slices

100 g (3½ oz) canned water chestnuts, sliced
    or quartered

2 spring onions, thinly sliced

2 tbsp chopped fresh coriander

6 eggs

2 garlic cloves, finely chopped

2 tsp finely chopped fresh root ginger

2 tbsp dry sherry

To finish

½ tsp toasted sesame oil

1½ tbsp Chinese bean sauce

1 tbsp balsamic vinegar

few drops of Chinese chilli sauce

fresh coriander leaves to garnish

Preparation time: 20 minutes

Cooking time: about 10 minutes

1 Preheat the grill to high. Mix the minced turkey with 1 tsp of the soy sauce, rubbing together with your fingers. Heat the oil in a heavy frying pan, about 26 cm (10½ in) in diameter, add the turkey and cook, breaking it up with a spoon, for 3–5 minutes or until it is lightly browned and crumbly. Add the Chinese leaves, bean sprouts, peas, smoked turkey or chicken, water chestnuts, spring onions and coriander, and stir-fry for 2–3 minutes.

2 Lightly beat the eggs with the garlic, ginger, sherry and remaining 1 tsp of soy sauce. Add to the pan, pouring the egg mixture evenly over the vegetables and turkey. Cook, stirring gently with a wooden spatula and lifting the sides of the omelette to let the uncooked egg mixture run onto the pan, until the omelette is set on the base. Slide the pan under the grill (keeping the handle away from the heat if it isn't ovenproof) and cook briefly to set the egg on top.

3 Meanwhile, mix together the sesame oil, bean sauce, balsamic vinegar and chilli sauce.

4 Cut the omelette into wedges and serve drizzled with the bean sauce mixture and garnished with coriander.

Plus points

- Eggs contain useful amounts of protein, which is essential for good health and well-being, plus vitamins A, B_2, B_{12}, E and niacin.
- Frozen vegetables often contain more vitamin C than fresh vegetables. For example, frozen peas retain 60–70% of their vitamin C content after freezing and maintain this level throughout storage.
- Chinese leaves are a good source of B vitamins, particularly folate, and of vitamin C.

Each serving provides

kcal 300, **protein** 28 g, **fat** 18 g (of which saturated fat 4 g), **carbohydrate** 5 g (of which sugars 3 g), **fibre** 1.5 g

✓✓✓	B_{12}, folate
✓✓	A, B_2, B_6, C, E, iron, zinc
✓	B_1, niacin, calcium, copper, potassium, selenium

Another idea

● For rolled Chinese omelettes filled with turkey meatballs, use 150 g (5½ oz) minced turkey mixed with 1½ tsp soy sauce; roll into 20 tiny meatballs. Brown lightly for 5–6 minutes, then remove from the pan with a draining spoon. Stir-fry all the vegetables in the frying pan (omit the smoked turkey or chicken). Heat 1 tsp sunflower oil in an 18 cm (7 in) omelette pan and pour in one-quarter of the egg mixture. Sprinkle one-quarter of the turkey meatballs and stir-fried vegetables over the top, then roll up as the egg mixture cooks and sets. The egg will tend to fall apart as the filling is heavy and the egg delicate, but just turn it, with the help of a palette knife. Make 4 omelettes in all. Serve with the dipping sauce, garnished with a sprinkling of chopped fresh coriander.

Chicken livers sautéed with sage

Chicken livers can be found fresh or frozen in most supermarkets and are an extremely economical standby ingredient to have in the freezer. The addition of a few well-chosen flavouring ingredients, like the fresh sage and balsamic vinegar used here, can transform the livers into something rather special.

Serves 4

8 rounds French bread

2 tbsp extra virgin olive oil

15 g (½ oz) butter

1 small red onion, finely chopped

2 garlic cloves, chopped

400 g (14 oz) chicken livers

225 g (8 oz) small chestnut or button
   mushrooms, quartered

3 tbsp balsamic vinegar

2 tbsp shredded fresh sage

salt and pepper

small sprigs of fresh sage to garnish

Preparation time: 5 minutes

Cooking time: 12–15 minutes

1 Preheat the oven to 180°C (350°F, gas mark 4). Arrange the French bread on a baking tray. Using 1 tbsp of the oil, lightly brush the slices of bread on the top side, then bake for 10 minutes or until golden brown.

2 Meanwhile, heat the remaining 1 tbsp of oil with the butter in a heavy-based frying pan. Add the onion and garlic, and sauté over a moderately high heat for 2–3 minutes or until softened.

3 Add the chicken livers and mushrooms, and cook, stirring constantly, to brown on all sides. As they cook, break up any large livers into bite-sized pieces, using the side of the spatula.

4 Add the balsamic vinegar, shredded sage and seasoning to taste. Reduce the heat a little and continue cooking for 5–10 minutes or until the livers are just cooked through.

5 Serve the chicken livers on top of the baked French bread rounds, garnished with sprigs of fresh sage.

Plus points

• Like all liver, chicken livers are a rich source of iron, necessary to help prevent anaemia.

• Garlic (along with leeks, onions and chives) contains allicin, which has anti-fungal and antibiotic properties. Garlic also contains other compounds which in animal studies have been shown to inactivate carcinogens and suppress the growth of tumours.

Some more ideas

• Serve on thick slices of toast rather than French bread, or with a celeriac and potato purée.

• For a Provençal version, replace the balsamic vinegar with 4 tbsp red wine and use 1 tsp dried herbes de Provence instead of the fresh sage. Serve with rice.

• The chicken livers can be baked instead of sautéed. Put all the ingredients in an ovenproof dish (melting the butter first) and mix together. (If preparing in advance, cover and refrigerate until ready to cook.) Place in the oven preheated to 220°C (425°F, gas mark 7) and bake for 12–15 minutes.

Each serving provides

kcal 315, **protein** 24 g, **fat** 12.5 g (of which saturated fat 4 g), **carbohydrate** 29 g (of which sugars 2 g), **fibre** 1.5 g

✓✓✓	A, B$_2$, B$_6$, B$_{12}$, folate, copper, iron
✓✓	B$_1$, C, niacin, selenium, zinc
✓	E

Chicken and sweet potato hash

This is a great supper dish to make with leftover roast chicken, or with turkey. Sweet potatoes are a colourful addition to the potatoes traditionally used in a hash, and sweetcorn adds a delightful texture. With its simple yogurt sauce, the hash needs only a crisp mixed salad and crusty, rustic bread to make a delicious meal.

Serves 4

300 g (10½ oz) potatoes, peeled

500 g (1 lb 2 oz) orange-fleshed sweet
   potatoes, peeled

225 g (8 oz) leeks, sliced

2 tbsp sunflower oil

225 g (8 oz) cooked chicken meat, without
   skin, diced

170 g (6 oz) frozen sweetcorn, thawed with
   boiling water and drained

8 sun-dried tomatoes packed in oil, drained
   and chopped

1 tsp paprika

salt

Yogurt-garlic sauce

150 g (5½ oz) plain low-fat yogurt

1 small garlic clove, crushed

½ tsp paprika

Preparation time: 10–15 minutes
Cooking time: 10–12 minutes

1 Cut the potatoes and sweet potatoes into small bite-sized chunks. Drop into a pan of boiling water, bring back to the boil and boil for 2 minutes. Add the leeks and cook for a further 1 minute. Drain well.

2 Heat the oil in a large non-stick frying pan and add the leeks and potatoes. Cook over a moderate heat, stirring frequently, for 3–4 minutes or until beginning to brown.

3 Add the chicken, sweetcorn, sun-dried tomatoes, paprika and salt to taste, and mix thoroughly. Continue cooking for 3–5 minutes, pressing down well to make a cake in the pan, and turning it over in chunks, until brown and crispy on both sides.

4 For the sauce, put the yogurt, garlic and paprika in a bowl and stir to mix. Serve portions of hash topped with the yogurt sauce.

Some more ideas

• Use 1 can sweetcorn, packed without sugar, about 200 g, well drained, instead of the frozen sweetcorn.

• To make a fruity, spicy chicken or turkey hash, chop 1 onion, 1 red pepper and 1 red-skinned dessert apple, and sauté together in the oil for 2 minutes. Then stir in 1 tbsp of your favourite curry spice blend and 2 tbsp sultanas or raisins. Add 550 g (1¼ lb) cooked potatoes and/or cooked sweet potatoes, cut into small bite-sized chunks, and cook over a moderate heat until beginning to brown. Mix in the cooked chicken or turkey together with 1 tbsp mango chutney, and finish cooking for 3–5 minutes, pressing into a cake and turning in chunks. Serve topped with Tzatziki (see page 140).

Plus points

• Sweet potatoes are an excellent source of beta-carotene, an antioxidant that helps to protect against heart disease and cancer. Sweet potatoes also provide good amounts of vitamin C and potassium, and contain more vitamin E than any other vegetable.

• Both potatoes and sweet potatoes are starchy carbohydrate foods, as are pasta, rice, bread and other grains. Starchy carbohydrates should make up almost half of the daily calorie intake in a healthy diet.

Each serving provides

kcal 460, protein 23 g, fat 18 g (of which saturated fat 3 g), carbohydrate 56 g (of which sugars 16 g), fibre 6 g

✓✓✓	A, B₆, C, E
✓✓	B₁, folate, copper, iron, potassium
✓	B₂, niacin, calcium, selenium, zinc

quick poultry dishes

86

quick poultry dishes

87

Main Course Poultry

Good dishes for every day and special days

A roast bird appeals to everyone, and there are lots of
roasting ideas here – chicken scented with fresh herbs
and garlic; turkey with a spicy couscous stuffing;
pheasant wrapped in Parma ham and cooked atop lentils
and dried apricots; duck with a Chinese glaze. Cooking
in casseroles and pot-roasts keeps poultry and game birds
beautifully moist, while poultry sausages and burgers
make a great change from red
meat varieties. Or for more exotic
flavours from around the world try
Mexican fajitas, Japanese teriyaki
grill, jambalaya or a spicy curry.

Roast herb and garlic chicken

Rather than rubbing butter over a bird before roasting, here a paste of fresh herbs and fromage frais is pushed under the skin. This keeps the roasting chicken beautifully moist as well as adding a wonderful flavour. The pan juices are used to make a simple sauce.

Serves 4

1 lemon

1 chicken, about 1.35 kg (3 lb), without giblets

15 g (½ oz) fresh coriander

15 g (½ oz) parsley

2 garlic cloves, peeled

2 tbsp fromage frais

150 ml (5 fl oz) dry white wine

salt and pepper

To garnish

lemon slices

sprigs of fresh coriander or parsley

Preparation time: 15 minutes
Cooking time: 1¾–2 hours

Each serving provides

kcal 229, **protein** 37 g, **fat** 6 g (of which saturated fat 2 g), **carbohydrate** 1 g (of which sugars 1 g), **fibre** 0 g

✓✓✓	B$_6$, B$_{12}$, niacin
✓✓	copper
✓	B$_1$, B$_2$, iron, potassium, selenium, zinc

1 Preheat the oven to 180°C (350°F, gas mark 4). Grate the zest from the lemon, then cut the lemon in half. Hold the chicken on end in a small roasting tin and squeeze the lemon juice inside the cavity (make sure that the juice doesn't run straight out of the other end). Push the lemon halves inside the cavity and sprinkle in half of the zest.

2 Place the chicken in the tin, breast side up. Very carefully ease your fingers under the skin, starting at the neck end. Loosen the skin over the breasts and thighs, without breaking it.

3 Combine the herbs and garlic in a blender or food processor and process until finely chopped. Add the fromage frais, remaining lemon zest and seasoning, and process again briefly to mix. (Alternatively, chop the herbs and garlic finely with a knife, then mix with the other ingredients.) Push the paste under the skin, easing it along so that it covers the breasts and thighs evenly in a thin layer. Secure the end of the neck skin by folding the wing tips under.

4 Cover the chicken with foil and roast for 45 minutes. Remove the foil and roast, uncovered, for a further 1–1¼ hours or until the juices run clear when a knife is inserted into the thickest part of the thigh. Baste once or twice with the juices in the tin.

5 Lift up the chicken, tipping it so that the juices can run out of the cavity into the tin. Set the chicken aside on a carving board to rest. Skim all the fat from the surface of the juices in the tin, then bring to the boil on top of the cooker. Add the white wine and bring back to the boil, scraping up all of the browned bits from the bottom of the tin. Boil the pan sauce for 1 minute. Season to taste.

6 Carve the chicken into slices or serving pieces. Garnish with lemon slices and sprigs of coriander or parsley, and serve with the pan sauce.

Plus points

• While the latest research shows that women should avoid alcohol altogether during pregnancy, in the population as a whole moderate alcohol consumption is now associated with a lower risk of death from coronary heart disease. Moderate means avoiding binges and taking no more than 3–4 units a day for men and 2–3 units a day for women.

• Some studies suggest that garlic may help to reduce high blood cholesterol levels and inhibit blood clotting, thereby reducing the risk of heart attack and stroke.

Some more ideas

• For a very simple roast chicken, just squeeze the lemon juice into the cavity and push in the lemon halves; omit the herb and fromage frais paste. Make the pan sauce with chicken stock, vegetable cooking water or even just with plain water, instead of wine.

• For an orange-scented roast chicken, stud an orange with 6 cloves, cut it in half and push the halves inside the cavity. Loosen the skin and push a mixture of 2 tbsp fromage frais and 2 tsp grated orange zest underneath, spreading it evenly over the breast and thighs. Make the pan sauce with red wine instead of white, plus the juice of 1 orange and 1 tbsp balsamic vinegar.

Roast turkey with lemon couscous

A small turkey like this is amazingly economical. It will give enough meat for at least 8 portions, or you can serve 4 people and have plenty of leftovers for sandwiches, salads and other dishes. Don't forget to keep the turkey carcass to make stock for soup (see page 28 for a delicious idea).

Serves 8

4 large lemons

340 g (12 oz) couscous

1 tsp turmeric

1 tsp ground cumin

1 tsp ground cinnamon

900 ml (1½ pints) hot chicken or turkey
  stock, preferably home-made (see page 23)

115 g (4 oz) ready-to-eat dried apricots,
  chopped

4 tbsp chopped fresh mint

1 turkey, about 2.25 kg (5 lb), without giblets

150 ml (5 fl oz) dry sherry

salt and pepper

sprigs of fresh mint to garnish

Preparation time: 20 minutes, plus 10 minutes
  soaking

Cooking time: about 1¾ hours

Each serving provides

kcal 310, **protein** 36 g, **fat** 4 g (of which saturated fat 1 g), **carbohydrate** 28 g (of which sugars 6.5 g), **fibre** 1 g

✓✓✓	B₆, B₁₂
✓✓	niacin, iron
✓	B₁, B₂, copper, potassium, zinc

1 Halve the lemons lengthways and squeeze out all the juice into a jug. Pull the membranes and pulp from each lemon half to leave a smooth clean shell. Cut a thin slice off the base of each shell so that it will stand firmly. Set aside.

2 Place the couscous in a medium-sized mixing bowl. Add 4 tbsp of the lemon juice, the spices, 750 ml (1¼ pints) of the stock, the apricots and mint, and stir to mix well. Leave to soak for 10 minutes or until the couscous has absorbed all the stock.

3 Preheat the oven to 200°C (400°F, gas mark 6). Place the turkey on a rack in a medium-sized roasting tin and pour over 150 ml (5 fl oz) hot water.

4 When the couscous is ready, use a spoon to stuff some of it into the neck end of the turkey (do not pack it in too firmly). Secure the skin flap underneath the bird with the wing tips. Spoon 2 tbsp of the lemon juice over the bird (freeze any remaining juice for use in other dishes). Cover the turkey loosely with oiled foil and roast for 1¾ hours. Baste the turkey with the roasting juices occasionally during cooking to keep it moist, and remove the foil for the last 30 minutes of cooking to allow the skin to brown. At the end of the cooking time, test the

turkey by pushing a metal skewer or thin knife into the thickest part of the thigh; the juices should run clear. If they are still pink, continue to roast the bird, testing every 10 minutes.

5 Meanwhile, fill the lemon halves with couscous, pressing down gently and mounding up the top. Spread the rest of the couscous in a small ovenproof dish and sit the filled lemon halves on top. Cover loosely with foil and place in the oven for the last 20 minutes of the turkey's roasting time, to heat through.

6 When the turkey is cooked, remove it from the tin and leave it to rest on a carving board for 10 minutes. Skim all the fat from the surface of the juices in the tin, then add the sherry and the remaining 150 ml (5 fl oz) stock. Bring to the boil on top of the cooker, scraping up the browned bits from the bottom of the tin. Boil for 5 minutes. Season to taste.

7 Carve the turkey and serve with the couscous-filled lemons, garnished with mint sprigs, the extra couscous and the pan sauce.

Some more ideas

• For a spicy Moroccan-style couscous stuffing, replace the apricots with 55 g (2 oz) each sultanas and toasted pine nuts. Use a mixture of chopped fresh coriander and flat-leaf parsley instead of mint. Omit the turmeric and add ½ tsp crushed dried chillies.

• Give the turkey a Mediterranean flavour by loosening the skin over the breast and inserting thin slices of lemon coated with a *'gremolata'* (the grated zest of 1 lemon, 2 garlic cloves, chopped, and 3 tbsp chopped parsley).

• Instead of the couscous mixture, try the stuffing recipes on pages 24–25.

Plus points

• Couscous is low in fat and high in starchy carbohydrate. It scores low on the Glycaemic Index scale, which means that it breaks down slowly in the body, releasing energy gradually into the bloodstream.

Pheasant with leeks and lentils

As pheasant has very little fat, wrapping it in Parma ham helps to prevent it from drying out, as well as adding flavour. For a healthy and delicious accompaniment, the birds are roasted on top of leeks and lentils.

Serves 4

2 pheasants, about 900 g (2 lb) each

½ orange, halved

1 onion, quartered

4 tsp Dijon mustard

4 sprigs of fresh sage

4 thin slices Parma ham

225 g (8 oz) Puy lentils

200 g (7 oz) leeks, sliced

2 sprigs of fresh thyme

1 garlic clove, crushed

75 g (2½ oz) ready-to-eat dried apricots, quartered

250 ml (8½ fl oz) dry cider

600 ml (1 pint) chicken stock, or more if needed, preferably home-made (see page 23)

To garnish

sprigs of fresh thyme and sage

1 orange, quartered

Preparation time: 20 minutes

Cooking time: 1 hour 20 minutes

Each serving provides

kcal 460, **protein** 49 g, **fat** 11 g (of which saturated fat 3.5 g), **carbohydrate** 40 g (of which sugars 12 g), **fibre** 8 g

✓✓✓	B₆, B₁₂, folate, copper, iron, selenium
✓✓	B₁, B₂, niacin, potassium, zinc
✓	C, calcium

1 Preheat the oven to 200°C (400°F, gas mark 6). Stuff each bird with a piece of orange and 2 onion quarters. Spread 2 tsp of mustard over the breast of each bird and top with a sprig of sage. Wrap with 2 slices of Parma ham and tie on with string.

2 Put the lentils into a large oval roasting dish with the leeks, the remaining 2 sage sprigs, the thyme sprigs, garlic and apricots. Set the pheasants on top and pour over the cider and 300 ml (10 fl oz) of the chicken stock. Roast for 40 minutes.

3 Heat the remaining stock to boiling and pour over the pheasants. Return to the oven to roast for a further 30–40 minutes, covering with foil to prevent the Parma ham from drying out.

4 Remove the birds from the lentils and test to see if they are cooked by piercing the leg with a sharp knife. The juices that run out should be clear; roast for a little longer if necessary. Set the pheasants aside to rest while you finish cooking the lentils.

5 Stir the lentil mixture. If it seems a little dry, add up to 150 ml (5 fl oz) more hot stock. Return to the oven to cook for a further 10–15 minutes or until the lentils are tender.

6 Carve the pheasants and serve on a bed of lentils, garnished with thyme and sage sprigs and orange wedges.

Plus points

- Puy lentils are an excellent source of fibre, particularly the soluble variety. They also provide useful amounts of many B vitamins and iron.
- Dried apricots offer good amounts of beta-carotene, which the body converts into vitamin A, plus potassium and soluble fibre. In addition, they are a useful source of iron, valuable for vegetarians, and of calcium.

Some more ideas

- Use 2 rashers of lean smoked back bacon instead of Parma ham. Stretch the rashers with the back of a knife to make them thin, then cut them in half crossways.
- For a more traditional roast pheasant, prepare the birds as above, but without the sage sprigs, and put in a roasting tin. Add 12 peeled shallots and 2 tbsp of olive oil to the tin. Roast as above for 1 hour 10 minutes. Meanwhile, make a bread sauce to serve with the roast. Finely chop 1 onion and put in a saucepan with 360 ml (12 fl oz) semi-skimmed milk, 6 whole cloves and 1 bay leaf. Bring slowly to the boil, then cover and simmer for 20 minutes or until the onion is completely tender. Beat in 115 g (4 oz) fine fresh white breadcrumbs and 1 tbsp chopped fresh tarragon. Season to taste. Serve the pheasants with the whole roast shallots and bread sauce on the side.

Chinese barbecued duck

Duck is notoriously fatty, but this method of cooking cuts down drastically on the amount of fat you eat with the meat. For a deliciously healthy meal start with a refreshing salad, then follow with the duck served with spicy or plain rice or noodles and stir-fried mixed vegetables with bean sprouts for extra colour and crunch.

Serves 4

1 duckling, about 2 kg (4½ lb), without giblets

2 tbsp hoisin sauce

2 tsp dried thyme

2 tsp five-spice powder

3 tbsp clear honey

3 tbsp dark soy sauce

Gingered sugarsnaps

225 g (8 oz) sugarsnap peas or mange-touts

grated zest of ½ orange

juice of 1 orange

1 tbsp coarsely grated fresh root ginger

2 tsp soy sauce

75 g (2½ oz) canned bamboo shoots, drained

1 tsp toasted sesame oil

Preparation time: 30 minutes, plus about
    5 hours drying
Cooking time: 1 hour

Each serving provides

kcal 265, protein 32 g, fat 8 g (of which saturated fat 2 g), carbohydrate 17 g (of which sugars 16.5 g), fibre 1.5 g

✓✓✓	B$_6$, B$_{12}$, C
✓✓	B$_1$, B$_2$, niacin, copper, iron, potassium, zinc
✓	folate

1 With poultry shears or a large knife, cut up one side of the duck's backbone, then cut out the backbone altogether. Trim off as much fat as you can and cut off the flaps of skin. Place the duck, skin side up, on the work surface and flatten with your hand. Prick the duck all over, piercing through the skin and fat but not into the meat.

2 Place the duck in a colander and pour boiling water over it a couple of times to release the fat. Dry the duck with kitchen paper. Push 2 metal skewers diagonally through the duck to keep it flat during cooking.

3 Mix together the hoisin sauce, thyme and five-spice powder, and spread on the underside of the duck. Place it, skin side up, on a rack set over a roasting tin. Put the honey, soy sauce and 300 ml (10 fl oz) of water in a small saucepan and bring to the boil. Pour this mixture over the duck, collecting the juices in the tin. Pour the mixture back over the duck twice more, then leave the duck, on the rack, in a cool, draughty place for about 5 hours. Alternatively, leave it in front of a fan, or in a fan oven with just the fan turned on and no heat, for 2 hours. The skin of the duck should dry out and look a bit like parchment paper. Reserve the honey and soy mixture.

4 Preheat the oven to 200°C (400°F, gas mark 6). Pour about 300 ml (10 fl oz) of water into the roasting tin. Roast for 1 hour or until the skin is very crisp and brown. If you don't like the spitting noises in the oven, lower the temperature to 180°C (350°F, gas mark 4) after 30 minutes, and increase the total cooking time by 10 minutes.

5 Meanwhile, bring the honey and soy mixture to the boil and reduce by half. Set this syrup aside.

6 About 10 minutes before the duck is ready, blanch the sugarsnap peas in boiling water for 2 minutes; drain and refresh under cold water. Put the orange zest and juice, ginger and soy sauce in a saucepan and bring to the boil. Add the sugarsnaps and bamboo shoots and heat for 1–2 minutes until the liquid is absorbed. Stir in the sesame oil.

7 Divide the duck into 4 portions and serve with the vegetables and the honey-soy syrup.

Plus points

● Sugarsnap peas provide good amounts of soluble fibre, which can help to lower high blood cholesterol levels. They are also a good source of vitamin C.

Some more ideas

• A more traditional way to prepare Cantonese duck is to keep it whole. Trim off the visible fat, then prick the skin all over (piercing through the fat but not into the meat). Plunge the duck into a large pan of boiling water and blanch for 1 minute. Drain and dry with kitchen paper.

Make the hoisin sauce mixture as above, also adding 1 tbsp coarsely grated fresh root ginger, 2 chopped spring onions, 2 tbsp dry sherry and 2 tbsp yellow bean sauce. Bring this mixture to the boil, then allow to cool before spooning it into the duck. Keep it inside the duck by tucking in the parson's nose, folding the flaps of skin

over and securing with wooden cocktail sticks. Pour the honey and soy mixture over the duck a few times, leave the duck to dry and then roast it on a rack for 1 hour. Spoon out the flavouring to serve with the duck.

• If you don't want to roast a whole duck, use leg portions or small boneless breasts.

French-style chicken in wine

Think of a French country-style meal and chances are your mind will conjure up the image of chicken simmering in robust red wine. This up-dated version of a classic bistro dish contains shallots, mushrooms and carrots, so the only accompaniment needed is potatoes – and, of course, lots of fresh French bread.

Serves 4

12 shallots or button onions

1½ tbsp garlic-flavoured olive oil

55 g (2 oz) back bacon, cut across into thin strips

12 chestnut or button mushrooms

4 chicken joints such as breasts, about 170 g (6 oz) each

several sprigs of parsley, stalks bruised

several sprigs of fresh thyme

1 bay leaf

150 ml (5 fl oz) chicken stock, preferably home-made (see page 23)

360 ml (12 fl oz) full-bodied red wine, such as Burgundy

300 g (10½ oz) carrots, cut into chunks

pinch of caster sugar

1 tbsp cornflour

salt and pepper

chopped parsley to garnish

Preparation time: 15 minutes

Cooking time: about 1¼ hours

Each serving provides

kcal 372, protein 37 g, fat 9 g (of which saturated fat 2 g), **carbohydrate 22 g** (of which sugars 7 g), **fibre 3 g**

✓✓✓	A, B₆, niacin, copper
✓✓	B₁, B₂, iron, potassium, selenium, zinc
✓	E, folate

A, B$_6$, niacin, copper

B$_1$, B$_2$, iron, potassium, selenium, zinc

E, folate

1 Put the shallots or onions in a heatproof bowl and pour over enough boiling water to cover. Leave for 30 seconds, then drain. When cool enough to handle, peel and set aside.

2 Heat 1 tbsp of the oil in a flameproof casserole. Add the bacon and fry for about 3 minutes, stirring often, until crispy. Remove with a draining spoon and set aside.

3 Add the shallots to the casserole and fry, stirring often, over a moderately high heat for 5 minutes or until browned all over. Remove with a draining spoon and set aside.

4 Add the mushrooms to the casserole, with the remaining ½ tbsp oil if needed, and fry for 3–4 minutes, stirring often, until golden.

5 Return half of the bacon and shallots to the casserole. Place the chicken joints on top and sprinkle with the remaining bacon and shallots. Tie the herbs into a bouquet garni and add to the casserole with the stock and wine. Season generously with pepper.

6 Bring to the boil, then reduce the heat to very low and simmer for 15 minutes. Add the carrots and continue simmering over a low heat for a further 30 minutes or until the chicken is cooked through and the carrots are tender but still crisp.

7 Lift out the chicken and arrange on a warmed serving platter. Strain the liquid into a saucepan. Add the bacon, mushrooms, shallots and carrots to the chicken and keep warm.

8 Put the bouquet garni back in the strained liquid, add the sugar and bring to the boil. Boil until the sauce is reduced to about 360 ml (12 fl oz). Mix the cornflour with a little water to make a smooth paste. Add to the sauce, stirring, and simmer until thickened. Adjust the seasoning to taste and discard the bouquet garni. Spoon the sauce over the chicken and vegetables, sprinkle with the parsley and serve.

Plus points

- Unlike most vegetables, which are most nutritious when eaten raw, cooking carrots increases their nutritional value. Because raw carrots have tough cell walls, the body can convert only about 25% of the beta-carotene present into vitamin A. Cooking breaks down the cell membrane, making it easier for the body to absorb and convert the beta-carotene.

- Red wine contains flavonoid compounds which may help to protect against heart disease.

Some more ideas

● If you cannot find garlic-flavoured olive oil, use extra virgin olive oil and fry 1 garlic clove, crushed, with the mushrooms.

● For chicken with Riesling, typical of the Alsace region of north-eastern France, take 550 g (1¼ lb) skinless boneless chicken breasts or thighs and cut into large chunks. Use Riesling instead of red wine. Add the carrots with the chicken and simmer for 30 minutes, then add 200 g (7 oz) frozen peas, straight from the freezer, and continue simmering for about 5 minutes.

Strain and reduce the cooking liquid as above, then thicken and enrich with 4 tbsp whipping cream or soured cream. Serve the chicken with egg noodles, boiled and tossed with finely chopped parsley or poppy seeds.

Marsala chicken with fennel

Cooking with a little wine – in this case the famous dessert wine from Sicily – gives great depth to a sauce: nearly all the alcohol and calories burn away, leaving behind only flavour. This sauce is thickened with a mixture of egg and lemon juice, which is typically Mediterranean and less rich than beurre manié or cream.

Serves 4

1 chicken, about 1.35 kg (3 lb), jointed

2 tbsp plain flour

2 tbsp extra virgin olive oil

1 large leek, coarsely chopped

1 tbsp chopped parsley

1 tsp fennel seeds

90 ml (3 fl oz) Marsala

500 ml (17 fl oz) chicken stock, preferably
    home-made (see page 23)

2 medium-sized bulbs of fennel, trimmed and
    cut into chunks

280 g (10 oz) shelled fresh or frozen peas

juice of 1 lemon

1 egg, lightly beaten

salt and pepper

To garnish

chopped parsley

shreds of lemon zest

Preparation time: 15 minutes
Cooking time: 45 minutes

Each serving provides

kcal 380, **protein** 46 g, **fat** 12 g (of which
saturated fat 2.5 g), **carbohydrate** 18 g (of
which sugars 5 g), **fibre** 5.5 g

✓✓✓	B$_6$, niacin
✓✓	B$_1$, B$_2$, C, folate, iron, potassium, selenium, zinc
✓	A, B$_{12}$, E, calcium, copper

1 Remove the skin from the chicken joints, except for any small pieces such as the wings which would be too difficult to skin. Season the flour and dust over the joints.

2 Heat 1 tbsp of the oil in a sauté pan and add the leek, parsley and fennel seeds. Cook over a moderate heat until the leek is softened, stirring frequently. Remove from the pan with a draining spoon and set aside.

3 Add the remaining 1 tbsp of oil to the pan and sauté the chicken for 6–7 minutes or until just golden all over. Remove the chicken from the pan and set aside. Pour in the Marsala and bubble until it is reduced to about 2 tbsp of glaze. Pour in the stock, and return the leek mixture and dark meat chicken joints and wings to the pan (wait to add the breasts as they can overcook). Add the chunks of fennel. Cover and simmer over a low heat for 10–15 minutes, then add the breasts and continue to cook, covered, for 15 minutes or until all the chicken joints are tender. Add the peas for the last 5 minutes of cooking.

4 Using a draining spoon, remove the chicken pieces and vegetables to a platter. Keep warm.

5 In a small bowl, mix the lemon juice into the egg. Slowly add about 4 tbsp of the hot cooking liquid to the lemon and egg mixture, stirring well, then slowly stir this mixture back into the liquid in the pan. Return the chicken and vegetables to the pan and gently warm it all through, taking care to ensure that the heat is very low so the sauce does not curdle into scrambled egg. Season to taste. Serve hot, garnished with parsley and shreds of lemon zest.

Plus points

● Bulb fennel contains more phytoestrogen than most vegetables. This naturally occurring plant hormone encourages the body to excrete excess oestrogen (a high level of oestrogen is linked with greater risk of breast cancer).

● Peas provide good amounts of the B vitamins B$_1$, B$_6$ and niacin. They also offer dietary fibre, particularly the soluble variety, plus some folate and vitamin C.

● The dark meat of chicken contains twice as much iron and zinc as the light meat.

Some more ideas

• Use 8 skinless boneless chicken thighs, about 500 g (1 lb 2 oz) in total, instead of a jointed chicken.

• Replace the leek with 2 chopped onions.

• For chicken with asparagus and fennel seeds, omit the peas and bulb fennel. Cut 1 bunch of asparagus (about 225 g/8 oz) into bite-sized pieces and add to the simmering chicken at the end of step 3, just before you remove the chicken joints and leeks. Thicken with the egg and lemon mixture, as above. Do not overcook the asparagus: 1–2 minutes should be enough. Asparagus is an excellent source of folate, and a good source of beta-carotene.

Pheasant casseroled with ginger

Casseroling is an excellent way to cook pheasant, as it produces succulent meat and a rich sauce. Cutting the bird into 8 pieces will allow each person to get a piece of breast as well as dark meat. Herby mashed potatoes, baby carrots and broccoli are good accompaniments for this aromatic dish.

Serves 4

1 large bulb of fennel, about 300 g
   (10½ oz)
1 tbsp sunflower oil
1 pheasant, about 1 kg (2¼ lb), jointed into
   4 or 8 pieces
100 g (3½ oz) shallots or button onions,
   halved
4 pieces stem ginger, about 115 g (4 oz) in
   total, cut into thin strips
4 tbsp ginger wine
300 ml (10 fl oz) chicken stock, preferably
   home-made (see page 23)
salt and pepper

Preparation time: 15 minutes
Cooking time: about 1¼ hours

1 Preheat the oven to 190°C (375°F, gas mark 5). Trim the fennel, retaining any feathery leaves for the garnish, then cut the bulb lengthways into 8 wedges. Set aside.

2 Heat the oil in a large flameproof casserole over a moderately high heat. Add the pheasant joints and shallots or button onions and fry to brown on all sides.

3 Add the fennel wedges. Turn the pheasant joints skin side up and sprinkle over the strips of ginger. Add the ginger wine and enough stock to come halfway up the pheasant joints but not cover them. Season to taste.

4 Bring to the boil, then cover the casserole and transfer to the oven. Cook for 1–1¼ hours or until the pheasant is tender. Serve garnished with the reserved fennel leaves.

Plus points

● Ginger is a useful alternative remedy for travel sickness or morning sickness. In herbal medicine it is used to aid digestion, to protect against respiratory and digestive infections, and to relieve flatulence.

● Pheasant is an excellent source of protein as well as iron and B vitamins. Although it is higher in fat than other game birds, most of this fat is monounsaturated.

Some more ideas

● Try a pheasant casserole with chestnuts and cabbage. Brown the pheasant joints and shallots, then add 200 g (7 oz) vacuum-packed chestnuts and 200 g (7 oz) red cabbage, cut into 4 wedges, instead of the fennel wedges. Replace the stem ginger with 2 tbsp marmalade and use red wine instead of ginger wine.

● Other game birds can be jointed and cooked in the same way.

● When game is out of season, use duck or chicken joints.

Each serving provides

kcal 235, **protein** 30 g, **fat** 11 g (of which saturated fat 3 g), **carbohydrate** 3.5 g (of which sugars 3 g), **fibre** 2 g

✓✓✓	B$_6$, B$_{12}$, niacin, iron
✓✓	B$_2$, potassium, zinc
✓	E, folate, calcium, copper

Pot-roasted partridge with sage

Naturally lean and low in calories, partridge is perfect for pot-roasting. The gentle cooking in cider and stock keeps this game bird moist, and fresh sage, pickled walnuts and apple add wonderful flavours. A carrot and celeriac purée is an ideal accompaniment, or try a potato mash with chopped spring onions.

Serves 4

4 partridges

15 g (½ oz) fresh sage

1 tbsp extra virgin olive oil

15 g (½ oz) butter

1 onion, finely chopped

1 tbsp plain flour

300 ml (10 fl oz) dry cider

150 ml (5 fl oz) chicken stock, preferably home-made (see page 23)

2 tsp German mustard

3 pickled walnuts, about 45 g (1½ oz) in total, thinly sliced

1 red-skinned dessert apple, cored and cut into thick slices

salt and pepper

Preparation time: 10 minutes

Cooking time: about 1¼ hours

Each serving provides

kcal 350, **protein** 43 g, **fat** 14 g (of which saturated fat 4.5 g), **carbohydrate** 9 g (of which sugars 5 g), **fibre** 1 g

✓✓✓	iron
✓	potassium

1 Preheat the oven to 160°C (325°F, gas mark 3). Tuck some sage sprigs into the body cavity of each partridge, reserving a few sprigs for garnish.

2 Heat the oil and butter in a flameproof casserole just large enough to hold the birds. Add the partridges and fry over a moderately high heat for 3–4 minutes, turning until evenly browned. Lift the birds out of the casserole and set aside.

3 Add the onion to the casserole and cook for 3 minutes, stirring, until lightly browned. Sprinkle in the flour and stir well to mix with the onion, then add the cider, stock, mustard and seasoning to taste. Bring to the boil, stirring constantly. Add the walnuts.

4 Return the partridges to the casserole, breast side down. Cover the casserole and transfer to the oven. Cook for 1 hour or until tender.

5 Lift the partridges out of the casserole and place on a warmed serving plate. Cover and keep hot.

6 Set the casserole on top of the cooker and boil the cooking liquid for 5 minutes or until reduced by one-third. Add the apple slices for the last 2 minutes of cooking.

7 Spoon the apple slices around the birds and garnish with the reserved sage sprigs. Serve with the sauce.

Some more ideas

● To make a carrot and celeriac purée, cook 340 g (12 oz) each peeled and diced celeriac and carrots in boiling water for 20 minutes or until very tender. Drain and mash, or purée in a food processor, with 3 tbsp semi-skimmed milk and seasoning to taste. Spoon into a serving dish and sprinkle with a little freshly grated nutmeg.

● For partridge pot-roasted with mushrooms, soak 15 g (½ oz) dried porcini mushrooms in 300 ml (10 fl oz) boiling water for 30 minutes. Drain, reserving the soaking liquid. Make the liquid up to 300 ml (10 fl oz) with the juice of 1 orange and chicken stock. Add 2 tsp tomato purée and 300 ml (10 fl oz) red wine. Use this as the cooking liquid. Replace the sage with fresh thyme, and add the soaked mushrooms instead of the pickled walnuts. Omit the apple, and garnish the dish with orange slices and a sprinkling of fresh thyme leaves.

Plus points

● Onions contain 2 compounds, allicin and sulphoraphane, which are believed to reduce the risk of cancer. Some studies suggest that these compounds may also help to reduce blood cholesterol levels and lessen the risk of blood clots forming, thus helping to prevent coronary heart disease.

Chicken and sausage jambalaya

A typical Cajun recipe, this is full of spicy, complex flavours. With lots of rice and vegetables, it is a great dish to make a small amount of meat go a long way, and offers a healthy balance of protein and carbohydrate.

Serves 6

300 g (10½ oz) skinless boneless chicken breasts (fillets)

2 tsp Cajun seasoning (see note below)

1 tsp dried sage or marjoram

2 tbsp sunflower oil

1 onion, sliced

1 green pepper, seeded and sliced

2 celery sticks, sliced

2 garlic cloves, crushed

400 g (14 oz) long-grain rice

1 litre (1¾ pints) chicken stock, preferably home-made (see page 23)

100 g (3½ oz) cooked smoked ham, cubed

100 g (3½ oz) chorizo or other spicy sausage, sliced

1 can Italian cherry tomatoes, or 1 can chopped tomatoes, about 400 g

Tabasco sauce, salt and pepper

To garnish

4–6 spring onions, trimmed and chopped

coarsely chopped parsley

Preparation time: 15 minutes
Cooking time: 35–40 minutes

Each serving provides

kcal 440, protein 22 g, fat 12 g (of which saturated fat 1.5 g), carbohydrate 58 g (of which sugars 4 g), fibre 1.5 g

✓✓✓	C
✓✓	B₆, E, iron
✓	niacin, copper, potassium, zinc

1 Cut the chicken into 2 cm (¾ in) cubes. Sprinkle with the Cajun seasoning and the sage or marjoram, making sure that the chicken is coated all over. Heat 1 tbsp of the oil in a large wide flameproof casserole or pan over a moderately high heat, add the chicken and fry for about 5 minutes, stirring frequently, until the cubes are browned on all sides. Remove from the pan with a draining spoon.

2 Add the remaining 1 tbsp of oil to the pan together with the onion, green pepper and celery, and fry for about 2 minutes, stirring. Add the garlic and rice, and stir and fry for another minute.

3 Pour in the stock and stir well. Return the chicken to the pan. Bring to the boil, then reduce the heat, cover and simmer for 15 minutes. Add the ham, sausage and canned tomatoes with their juice. Cook, covered, for a further 5–10 minutes or until the rice has absorbed all the liquid.

4 Season to taste with Tabasco sauce, salt and pepper. Serve hot, sprinkled with the chopped spring onions and parsley.

Some more ideas

● If you cannot find ready-made Cajun seasoning, use a mixture of 1½ tsp paprika and ½ tsp cayenne pepper.

● Use brown rice instead of white rice. It will take 5–10 minutes longer to cook and may need more liquid. Brown rice retains the nutritious high-fibre bran coating that is removed from white rice.

● Instead of Tabasco, you can use 2 tsp chilli sauce. If you like a stronger tomato flavour, add 1 tbsp tomato purée with the tomatoes.

● Add some white wine in place of some of the stock – 150 ml (5 fl oz) will give a good flavour.

● For a chicken and prawn jambalaya, leave out the smoked ham and spicy sausage and add 200 g (7 oz) peeled raw tiger prawns instead. Also add extra vegetables – 100 g (3½ oz) each frozen green beans and frozen peas. Add these 10 minutes before the end of cooking.

Plus points

● Green pepper provides vitamin C and beta-carotene, both of which have strong protective antioxidant functions against cancer, heart disease and stroke.

● Even when used in moderation, sunflower oil provides good amounts of vitamin E, which is a powerful antioxidant, protecting cell membranes from damage by free radicals. Other good sources of vitamin E include sunflower seeds and other oils derived from vegetables and nuts.

Chicken and potato curry

Letting the chicken pieces sit for half an hour in a gingery marinade makes all the difference to this curry. Skinning the chicken not only does away with most of the bird's fat, it also lets the spicy flavours really permeate the flesh. Potatoes make a great addition, adding bulk to the curry.

Serves 4

1 chicken, about 1.35 kg (3 lb), jointed into 8 pieces
½ tsp turmeric
4 cm (1½ in) piece fresh root ginger, peeled and finely chopped
juice of ½ lemon
2 tbsp sunflower oil
1 dried red chilli, broken into 2–3 pieces
1 tsp brown or black mustard seeds
½ tsp fennel seeds
¼ tsp cumin seeds
¼ tsp ground cumin
¼ tsp ground cinnamon
1 tbsp chickpea flour (gram flour)
3 garlic cloves, roughly crushed
½ green pepper, thinly sliced
1 large onion, sliced
1 can chopped tomatoes, about 400 g
250 g (9 oz) potatoes, peeled
¼ green cabbage, about 140 g (5 oz), thinly sliced
140 g (5 oz) frozen peas, thawed with boiling water and drained
salt and pepper

Preparation time: 30 minutes, plus 30 minutes marinating
Cooking time: 45 minutes

1 Remove the skin from the chicken joints. Cut 3–4 slashes in the flesh of each joint, right to the bone. Rub the turmeric, ginger, lemon juice and a little salt all over the chicken joints, then leave to marinate for about 30 minutes.

2 Heat the oil in a large, heavy-based frying pan. Add the dried chilli, mustard seeds, fennel seeds and cumin seeds, and let them sputter and pop for a few minutes. Stir in the ground cumin, cinnamon and chickpea flour. Watch carefully to be sure you do not burn the spices, as this can happen very quickly.

3 Add the garlic, green pepper and onion to the spice mixture and cook for a few minutes, stirring. Add the chicken and tomatoes and stir to mix. Cover and cook for 15 minutes.

4 Meanwhile, cook the potatoes in boiling water for 5 minutes; drain and cut into bite-sized pieces. Blanch the cabbage in a separate pan of boiling water for 1 minute, then drain.

5 Add the potatoes and cabbage to the curried chicken and stir in. Cover the pan again and continue to simmer over a moderately low heat for 20–25 minutes or until the chicken is completely cooked and tender. Add the peas and warm through for a few minutes. Serve hot, with Indian breads and pickles.

Plus points

• Traditional favourite vegetables, such as the humble potato, are a useful source of vitamin C. At one time they were very important in preventing scurvy in Britain during the winter months. Eaten frequently, potatoes can still contribute significant vitamin C to the diet, with antioxidant properties that play an important role in the prevention of cancer and heart disease.

• The vitamin C provided by the peas, tomatoes and potatoes will increase the absorption of iron from the chicken.

• All the water-soluble vitamins from the vegetables – vitamin C from the peas, tomatoes and potatoes, and B vitamins from the peas – are retained in the sauce of this curry.

Each serving provides

kcal 350, **protein** 39 g, **fat** 11 g (of which saturated fat 2 g), **carbohydrate** 26 g (of which sugars 10 g), **fibre** 6 g

✓✓✓	B_6, C, niacin
✓✓	B_1, E, folate, copper, iron, potassium
✓	A, calcium, selenium, zinc

Some more ideas

● Make this the day before you want to eat it – the curry is even better when the flavours have had longer to soak into the potatoes.

● For a hotter, more garlicky curry, use 2 dried red chillies and up to 8 garlic cloves. Eating a lot of garlic may help to lower blood pressure.

● For a chicken and broccoli curry with yogurt, omit the potatoes, cabbage and peas, and instead use 2 medium-sized bunches of broccoli, about 450 g (1 lb) in total. Separate the heads into florets; peel the stalks and cut into bite-sized chunks. Blanch both florets and stalk chunks in boiling water for 2 minutes, then drain and refresh in cold water. Add the broccoli during the last 5–10 minutes of cooking the chicken. Just before serving, stir 3 tbsp plain low-fat yogurt into the sauce. Serve this curry with rice. Broccoli contains phytochemicals and antioxidants that offer protection against cancer and other diseases.

Turkey mole

This is a simplified, quite mild version of the classic spicy-hot Mexican recipe, made with lean turkey, raisins and almonds. The surprising – yet traditional – ingredient added towards the end of the cooking time is bitter chocolate, which enriches and darkens the sauce. Serve with boiled rice and a salad.

Serves 4

2 tbsp sunflower oil

1 large onion, chopped

2 garlic cloves, crushed

1 fresh red chilli, seeded and sliced (optional)

2 tbsp sesame seeds

500 g (1 lb 2 oz) skinless turkey breast steaks, cut into thin strips

1½ tbsp mild chilli powder, or more to taste

½ tsp ground cloves

1 can chopped tomatoes, about 400 g

85 g (3 oz) raisins

150 ml (5 fl oz) chicken stock, preferably home-made (see page 23)

15 g (½ oz) dark chocolate, chopped

4 tbsp toasted flaked almonds

2 tbsp chopped fresh coriander

salt and pepper

sprigs of fresh coriander to garnish

Preparation time: 10 minutes
Cooking time: 25 minutes

Each serving provides

kcal 435, **protein** 35 g, **fat** 22 g (of which saturated fat 3.5 g), **carbohydrate** 26 g (of which sugars 24 g), **fibre** 4 g

✓✓✓	B₆, B₁₂, E, copper
✓✓	C, niacin, iron, potassium, zinc
✓	B₁, B₂, folate

1 Heat the oil in a large wide pan over a moderately low heat. Add the onion and garlic with the sliced chilli and sesame seeds and cook, stirring frequently, for 10 minutes or until the onion is soft and golden.

2 Add the strips of turkey and stir them briefly round the pan to mix with the onion. Sprinkle over the chilli powder and cloves, and add the canned tomatoes with their juice and the raisins. Stir well to mix.

3 Pour in the stock. Bring to the boil, then reduce the heat to low, cover the pan and leave to simmer gently for 10 minutes.

4 Add the chocolate, almonds and chopped coriander, and stir until the chocolate has melted. Season to taste. Spoon into a serving dish, garnish with sprigs of coriander and serve immediately.

Some more ideas

• Diced cooked turkey can be used as an alternative to the raw turkey. Add to the sauce with the raisins.

• To make turkey *mole* tacos, mix 1 tsp cornflour with 1 tbsp cold water and stir into the sauce before the chocolate in step 4. Bubble, stirring, until thickened, then add the chocolate, almonds and coriander. Make a salad with 1 red onion, thinly sliced, 2 tomatoes, chopped, 1 large avocado, sliced, a wedge of iceberg lettuce, shredded, and a handful of fresh coriander leaves. Heat 12 taco shells in the oven preheated to 180ºC (350ºF, gas mark 4) for 3 minutes or according to the instructions on the packet. To serve, place a little salad in the warmed taco shells, then spoon over the turkey *mole*. Eat with your fingers.

Plus points

• Research has shown that lycopene – the natural pigment that gives tomatoes their red colour – can reduce the risk of heart disease and prostate cancer. A 6-year study of 48,000 men, conducted at Harvard medical school, found that consuming tomato products more than twice a week was associated with a reduced risk of prostate cancer of up to 34%. Processed tomatoes – canned tomatoes, tomato purée and so on – contain much higher concentrations of lycopene than fresh.

• Raisins contain a useful amount of fibre and potassium.

Chicken and rosemary cobbler

This deep-dish pie has an Italian-style filling of succulent chunks of chicken, sliced peppers, mushrooms and black olives in a tomato sauce, and is topped with fresh rosemary scone wedges. A crunchy raw vegetable salad would be a good accompaniment to complete the meal.

Serves 6

1 chicken, about 1.1 kg (2½ lb)

2 sprigs of fresh rosemary

1 bay leaf

1 tbsp sunflower oil

1 onion, sliced

1 garlic clove, chopped

2 green peppers, seeded and thickly sliced

170 g (6 oz) button mushrooms, quartered

2 cans chopped tomatoes, 400 g each

2 tbsp medium dry sherry (optional)

115 g (4 oz) stoned black olives

pepper

Rosemary scone topping

100 g (3½ oz) self-raising white flour

100 g (3½ oz) self-raising wholemeal flour

¼ tsp salt

1 tsp baking powder

2 tsp chopped fresh rosemary

30 g (1 oz) butter

100 ml (3½ fl oz) semi-skimmed milk

Preparation time: 1½ hours, plus cooling
Cooking time: 10-15 minutes

Each serving provides

kcal 340, **protein** 24 g, **fat** 13 g (of which saturated fat 5 g), **carbohydrate** 33 g (of which sugars 9 g), **fibre** 5 g

✓✓✓	B₆, C, copper
✓✓	E, folate, niacin, iron, potassium
✓	A, B₁, B₂, calcium, selenium, zinc

1 Put the chicken in a large saucepan with the rosemary sprigs and bay leaf. Cover with water and bring to the boil, then reduce the heat and simmer for 1 hour or until tender.

2 Remove the chicken from the liquid. When cool enough to handle, take the meat from the carcass, discarding all the skin. Cut the meat into bite-sized chunks and set aside.

3 Heat the oil in a large saucepan. Add the onion, garlic, peppers and mushrooms, and cook for 5 minutes, stirring occasionally, until the onion is beginning to brown. Stir in the canned tomatoes with their juice, the sherry and olives, and season with pepper. Remove from the heat and set aside.

4 Preheat the oven to 230°C (450°F, gas mark 8).

5 To make the scone topping, put the white and wholemeal flours, salt, baking powder, chopped rosemary and pepper to taste in a bowl. Mix together, then rub in the butter until the mixture resembles fine crumbs. Make a well in the centre and add the milk. Mix to make a fairly soft, but not sticky, dough, adding more milk if necessary. Transfer the dough to a floured surface and knead briefly, then roll out to a round about 1 cm (½ in) thick and 18 cm (7 in) in diameter. Cut into 6 wedges.

6 Add the chunks of chicken to the vegetable mixture. Put the saucepan back on the heat and bring to the boil, then simmer for 2–3 minutes to reheat, stirring occasionally. Transfer to a 2 litre (3½ pint) deep pie dish.

7 Arrange the rosemary scone wedges on top of the chicken filling and brush them with a little extra milk, if wished. Bake for 10–15 minutes or until the scone wedges are risen and golden brown. Serve hot.

Plus points

- Wholemeal flour is an excellent source of many of the B vitamins, as well as iron and zinc. It also provides dietary fibre, particularly the insoluble variety.

- Peppers are packed with vitamin C – weight for weight they offer twice as much vitamin C as oranges. They are also rich in beta-carotene, which the body converts into vitamin A.

main course poultry

Some more ideas

- Replace the suggested vegetables with alternatives such as sliced celery, sliced carrots and diced aubergine.
- Use yellow or red peppers instead of green ones, for a sweeter taste.
- For a polenta topping, slice half a 1 kg packet of ready-made polenta into 12 discs. Arrange them, overlapping, on top of the chicken filling and brush lightly with a little extra virgin olive oil. Bake for 10–15 minutes or until beginning to brown.
- The chicken poaching broth (see step 1) can be used as the base for a soup.
- Replace the canned tomatoes with a sauce based on the poaching broth. Mix 3 tbsp cornflour with a little cold water. Bring 450 ml (15 fl oz) of the strained broth to the boil and whisk in the cornflour mixture. Simmer, stirring, until thickened. Whisk in 2 tbsp tomato purée, the sherry and olives. Season to taste.

Turkey drumsticks braised with baby vegetables

This is a simple dish to prepare and makes an economical, healthy mid-week family meal, low in calories and fat. Roasted in the French style, in stock with a few herbs, the meat from the turkey legs turns out wonderfully moist and tender. Serve with baked or mashed potatoes to add starchy carbohydrate.

Serves 4

2 tbsp sunflower oil

4 medium leeks, thickly sliced

12 baby carrots

12 baby courgettes

12 baby corn

300 ml (10 fl oz) turkey or chicken stock,
    preferably home-made (see page 23)

2 sprigs of fresh rosemary

1 bay leaf

2 large turkey drumsticks, about 600 g
    (1 lb 5 oz) each, skinned

pepper

Preparation time: 10 minutes

Cooking time: 1½ hours

Each serving provides

kcal 250, **protein** 32 g, **fat** 10 g (of which saturated fat 2 g), **carbohydrate** 9 g (of which sugars 8 g), **fibre** 6 g

✓✓✓	A, B$_6$, B$_{12}$, C, folate
✓✓	B$_1$, E, niacin, iron, potassium, zinc
✓	B$_2$, calcium, copper

1 Preheat the oven to 200°C (400°F, gas mark 6). Heat the oil in a large flameproof casserole over a moderately high heat. Add the leeks, carrots, courgettes and baby corn, and fry for 3–4 minutes, stirring all the time, until beginning to brown.

2 Pour in the stock, and add the rosemary and bay leaf. Season the turkey drumsticks with pepper and put on top of the vegetables.

3 Transfer to the oven and braise for about 1½ hours or until the turkey is golden brown and cooked. Baste the turkey about halfway through the cooking, and stir the vegetables round a bit. Test by piercing the thickest part of a drumstick with a sharp knife; the juices that run out should be clear.

4 Carve the meat from the turkey drumsticks into slices. Serve with the vegetables and a little of the stock spooned over.

Some more ideas

• Instead of turkey drumsticks, use 8 chicken drumsticks. Braise for about 1 hour.

• Replace 150 ml (5 fl oz) of the stock with the same quantity of white wine.

• Use 4 large carrots and 4 large courgettes, all cut into 5 cm (2 in) chunks, instead of the baby vegetables.

• Roast the turkey on a bed of root vegetables: include the carrots, but replace the leeks, courgettes and baby corn with 12 baby parsnips, 12 baby turnips and ½ small swede, cut into thick fingers. Or use 4 large carrots, parsnips and turnips with the swede, and cut all the vegetables into chunks.

Plus points

• Carrots may be one of the earliest foods eaten by man. Native to Asia, they were being cultivated long before the birth of Christ. The beta-carotene found in carrots is much better absorbed by the body (and converted into vitamin A) after the carrots have been cooked, and even more so if they are eaten along with a little fat or oil.

• Sweetcorn provides useful amounts of fibre and vitamin A (from beta-carotene).

main course poultry

114

Barbecued chicken

Because the flavour of chicken is quite mild, it benefits from a tasty baste when barbecued or grilled, and this also helps to keep the outside from burning until the chicken is cooked through – especially when cooking over charcoal. This recipe is for a spicy Jamaican jerk baste, and there are four more deliciously different ideas.

Serves 4

8 chicken drumsticks or thighs, about 675 g (1½ lb) in total

lime wedges to garnish

Jamaican jerk baste

3 tbsp extra virgin olive oil

1 onion, very finely chopped

2 garlic cloves, finely chopped

1 fresh red chilli, seeded and finely chopped

½ tsp salt

½ tsp ground allspice

¼ tsp ground cinnamon

grated zest and juice of 1 lime

Preparation time: 20 minutes, plus at least 1 hour marinating

Cooking time: 20-25 minutes

Each serving provides

kcal 260, **protein** 33 g, **fat** 13 g (of which saturated fat 3 g), **carbohydrate** 3 g (of which sugars 2 g), **fibre** 0.5 g

✓✓✓ B₁₂, niacin

✓ copper, iron, potassium, selenium, zinc

1 To make the baste, heat the oil in a small frying pan over a moderately low heat. Add the onion, garlic and chilli and cook, stirring frequently, for about 10 minutes or until the onion is softened and starting to brown. Sprinkle over the salt.

2 Tip into a large shallow bowl. Add the spices and the lime zest and juice, and stir well to mix.

3 Remove the skin from the chicken pieces. Make a few shallow slashes in the meat of each piece, then add to the bowl. Turn the pieces to coat thoroughly with the baste, rubbing it into the slashes in the meat. Cover and leave to marinate at room temperature for 1 hour or in the fridge for up to 24 hours.

4 Prepare a charcoal fire. When it has burned down to coals covered with grey ash, remove the chicken pieces from the marinating baste and barbecue them for 20–25 minutes, turning and brushing frequently with the baste, until cooked all the way through.

5 Alternatively, preheat the grill to moderately high. Arrange the chicken pieces on the grill rack and grill for 20–25 minutes, turning and basting frequently.

6 Serve the chicken hot, garnished with lime wedges.

Some more ideas

• For an American barbecue baste, fry the onion and garlic in the oil, then add 4 tbsp tomato ketchup, 2 tbsp Worcestershire sauce, 2 tbsp red wine vinegar and 2 tbsp molasses or treacle.

• For a New Orleans baste, fry the onion and garlic in the oil, then add the lime zest and juice, 150 g (5½ oz) plain low-fat yogurt, 3 tbsp chopped parsley and 2 tbsp Cajun seasoning (see page 106).

• For a red wine and thyme baste, fry the onion and garlic in the oil with 2 fresh bay leaves and 1 tbsp fresh thyme leaves. Add 175 ml (6 fl oz) red wine and ½ tsp coarse black pepper.

• For a maple syrup and orange baste, fry the onion and garlic in the oil, then add the salt, 3 tbsp maple syrup, the grated zest and juice of 1 orange, 1 tbsp snipped fresh chives and 1 tbsp chopped fresh tarragon.

Plus points

• Chillies are richer in vitamin C than citrus fruit, although to benefit from this you would have to eat a lot of them.

• The Mediterranean diet is thought to be much healthier than the average UK diet. One of the reasons for this is the use of olive oil, a monounsaturated fat, rather than butter and other saturated fats.

117

Teriyaki grilled poussin

Once spatchcocked (split open and flattened), poussins can be quickly grilled, each bird then providing a single serving. Here they are basted with a Japanese-style mixture made with fresh ginger, soy sauce and sesame oil. Serve with boiled jasmine rice or noodles and crisp, steamed vegetables such as Chinese leaf and mange-tout.

Serves 2

2 poussins, about 400 g (14 oz) each

red chillies to garnish (optional)

Teriyaki baste

2 garlic cloves, crushed

1 tbsp finely grated fresh root ginger

1 tbsp clear honey

2 tbsp toasted sesame oil

2 tbsp dark soy sauce

½ tsp very finely chopped fresh red chilli,
    or to taste

Preparation time: 15 minutes, plus 30 minutes
    marinating

Cooking time: 30 minutes

Each serving provides

kcal 345, **protein** 40 g, **fat** 16.5 g (of which saturated fat 3 g), **carbohydrate** 10 g (of which sugars 9 g), **fibre** 0 g

✓✓✓	B₆, niacin
✓✓	copper, potassium
✓	iron, selenium, zinc

1 To spatchcock the poussins, use a knife or poultry shears to cut up one side of the backbone, then cut out the backbone altogether. Open out each bird on a chopping board, skin side up, and press down firmly with the palm of your hand. Cut off the wing tips and knuckles to make the birds a neater shape, then carefully remove the skin. Secure each bird in a flat position with a long metal skewer, pushing it through crossways from the meaty part of one drumstick to the other. Place the birds in a large shallow dish or roasting tin.

2 Mix together the teriyaki baste ingredients, then pour over the poussins, turning so they are well coated on both sides. Set aside to marinate for at least 30 minutes.

3 Preheat the grill to moderate. Place the poussins on the grill rack, skinned side down. Grill for about 30 minutes – basting frequently with the teriyaki mixture and turning over after 15 minutes – until cooked through. Test by piercing the thigh with the tip of a knife; the juices that run out should be clear.

4 While the poussins are cooking, make the chillies into 'flowers', if using, by slicing one end of each chilli into fine 'petals'. Serve the poussins hot, garnished with the chilli flowers.

Plus points

• Some studies have shown that chillies can help to reduce blood cholesterol levels. There are also reports suggesting that eating chillies can help to protect against gastric ulcers by causing the stomach lining to secrete a mucus which coats the stomach, thus protecting it from damage by irritants such as aspirin or alcohol.

• Removing the skin from chicken reduces its fat content considerably. If this is done before cooking, and then an oil-based baste is used to add flavour and moisture, the fat is still kept low.

Some more ideas

• To make a tomato and cumin baste for the poussins, replace the ginger and soy sauce with 2 tbsp tomato ketchup and 1 tbsp Worcestershire sauce, and add 1 tsp Dijon mustard and ¼ tsp cumin seeds. Omit the chilli.

• Use 4 skinless boneless chicken breasts (fillets) instead of the poussins, to serve 4. Double the ingredients for the teriyaki baste, except the toasted sesame oil, and grill for 10–12 minutes.

main course poultry

Chicken goujons with mustard dip

A favourite with both adults and children, this is a simple healthy version of the popular deep-fried take-away snack. Served hot, with oven chips and fresh vegetables, it makes a good family meal. Served cold, the goujons are ideal for a picnic or a packed lunch.

Serves 4

150 ml (5 fl oz) soured cream

7 tbsp wholegrain mustard

1 tbsp snipped fresh chives

550 g (1¼ lb) skinless boneless chicken breasts (fillets)

2 tbsp plain flour

200 g (7 oz) fresh wholemeal breadcrumbs

1 garlic clove, crushed (optional)

1 tbsp paprika

2 eggs

pepper

lemon or lime wedges to serve

Preparation time: 25 minutes, plus 30 minutes chilling

Cooking time: 30–40 minutes

Each serving provides

kcal 462, **protein** 43 g, **fat** 19 g (of which saturated fat 7 g), **carbohydrate** 31 g (of which sugars 3.5 g), **fibre** 4.5 g

✓✓✓	B₆, niacin
✓✓	A, B₁₂, copper, iron, selenium, zinc
✓	B₁, B₂, folate, calcium, potassium

1 To make the mustard dip, mix together the soured cream, 1 tbsp of the mustard, the chives and pepper to taste. Spoon into a small serving bowl. Cover and chill until required.

2 Meanwhile, split open each chicken breast horizontally, then cut lengthways into thin strips. Put the flour in a large polythene bag, add the chicken strips and shake the bag until all the strips are coated in flour.

3 Put the breadcrumbs, garlic, if using, the remaining 6 tbsp of mustard and the paprika in a large bowl, and mix together until well blended. Tip the mixture onto a large plate. Break the eggs onto a deep plate and lightly beat with a fork.

4 Remove the chicken strips, one at a time, from the bag of flour, shaking off any excess, and dip first into the beaten egg and then into the breadcrumb mixture, pressing the breadcrumbs evenly over them. Arrange the goujons on a large non-stick baking tray and chill for about 30 minutes.

5 Preheat the oven to 200°C (400°F, gas mark 6).

6 Bake the chicken goujons for 30–40 minutes or until they are golden brown and crisp. Serve hot or cold, with the mustard dip and with lemon or lime wedges.

Some more ideas

• For curry-flavoured goujons, replace the mustard in both the chicken coating and dip with curry paste (mild or medium, to taste).

• For spicier goujons, omit the mustard and add ½ tsp ground cardamom, ½ tsp ground cinnamon, 1 tsp ground cumin and 2 tsp ground coriander to the breadcrumbs.

• To make oven chips, scrub 675 g (1½ lb) baking potatoes and cut into thick chips. Toss in a polythene bag with 1 tbsp sunflower oil and seasoning to taste, to coat the chips lightly. Heat a baking tray in the oven preheated to 200°C (400°F, gas mark 6). Spread the chips in a single layer on the hot baking tray and bake for 20 minutes. Stir and turn them over, then bake for a further 40 minutes or until tender, crisp and browned, turning occasionally.

Plus points

• Soured cream is surprisingly low in fat compared with other creams, but still gives a rich taste and creamy texture – 1 level tbsp soured cream contains 2.85 g fat and 30 kcal, whereas the same quantity of whipping cream has 5.85 g fat and 56 kcal.

• Wholemeal breadcrumbs offer considerably more fibre than white breadcrumbs (5.8 g fibre per 100 g/3½ oz as compared to 1.5 g).

Turkey roulades

Fresh spinach, roasted red peppers, ricotta cheese and a touch of Parmesan together make a fantastic filling for tender turkey roulades – rolled-up breast escalopes. Braised in stock and vermouth, and served with asparagus, this makes an elegant, attractive dish for a special occasion meal.

Serves 4

4 skinless turkey breast steaks, about
   140 g (5 oz) each
140 g (5 oz) fresh spinach leaves
1 small red pepper, seeded and quartered
140 g (5 oz) ricotta cheese
1 egg, beaten
2 tbsp freshly grated Parmesan cheese
2 tbsp fresh white breadcrumbs
2 tbsp chopped fresh basil
pinch of freshly grated nutmeg
150 ml (5 fl oz) dry vermouth
150 ml (5 fl oz) chicken stock, preferably
   home-made (see page 23)
4 tbsp crème fraîche
225 g (8 oz) thin asparagus spears

Preparation time: 30 minutes
Cooking time: 35 minutes

Each serving provides
kcal 418, **protein** 45 g, **fat** 16 g (of which
saturated fat 9 g), **carbohydrate** 14 g (of
which sugars 8 g), **fibre** 2.5 g

✓✓✓	A, B$_6$, B$_{12}$, C, folate, niacin
✓✓	B$_2$, calcium, copper, iron, potassium, zinc
✓	B$_1$, E

1 Put each turkey steak between 2 sheets of cling film and, with a rolling pin, bat them out into rough squares about 5 mm (¼ in) thick. Set these turkey escalopes aside.

2 Place the spinach in a large pan, with just the water clinging to the leaves after washing, cover and cook for 2 minutes or until wilted. Drain well, squeezing out all excess liquid, then chop finely and put into a large bowl.

3 Preheat the grill. Arrange the red pepper quarters, skin side up, on the grill rack and grill for 6 minutes or until the skin is charred. Transfer the peppers to a polythene bag and seal. Leave until cool enough to handle, then peel and dice.

4 Add the red pepper to the spinach together with the ricotta cheese, beaten egg, Parmesan, breadcrumbs, basil and nutmeg. Season to taste. Mix well. Divide the filling among the turkey escalopes, spreading it over them evenly. Roll up each one, folding in the sides to enclose the filling, and secure with wooden cocktail sticks.

5 Put the roulades in a frying pan or sauté pan that will hold them comfortably and pour over the vermouth and chicken stock. Cover tightly and bring to the boil, then reduce the heat and simmer for 20 minutes.

6 Remove the roulades from the pan and keep hot. Bring the cooking liquid back to the boil and boil until reduced to 150 ml (5 fl oz). Stir in the crème fraîche and boil for a further 1–2 minutes or until slightly thickened. Adjust the seasoning to taste.

7 While the liquid is reducing, cook the asparagus spears in boiling water for 2–3 minutes or until just tender. Drain, refresh with cold water and keep warm.

8 Remove and discard the cocktail sticks from the turkey roulades, then cut into neat slices. Serve garnished with the asparagus spears and with the sauce drizzled round.

Plus points

• Compared with most other cheeses, ricotta is relatively low in fat. It is a good source of protein, calcium, and vitamins B$_2$ and B$_{12}$. Mixing bland ricotta with a little Parmesan cheese is a good way to add flavour without increasing the fat too much.

• Asparagus is a rich source of many of the B vitamins, especially folate. New research suggests that folate may have a role in helping to protect against heart disease.

Another idea

• For turkey roulades with braised peppers, make the stuffing as above but without the red peppers. Heat 2 tbsp extra virgin olive oil in a frying pan or sauté pan and brown the roulades all over. Remove from the pan and set aside. Add 1 large red pepper and 1 large yellow pepper, both seeded and thickly sliced, to the pan and cook for 4–5 minutes or until beginning to soften. Add 6 garlic cloves, peeled and left whole, and 1 red onion, cut into wedges, and soften for 2 minutes. Add 2 plum tomatoes, each cut into 6 wedges, 1 tbsp chopped fresh rosemary and 12 pitted black olives and stir well to mix with the peppers and onion. Put the roulades on top of the vegetables and pour over 90 ml (3 fl oz) chicken stock or white wine. Cover and simmer for 20 minutes, turning the roulades once. Remove the cocktail sticks and cut each roulade in half diagonally. Serve on top of the braised peppers.

Basil-stuffed chicken breasts

This stylish-looking main course is surprisingly easy to make. The chicken breasts can be prepared in advance, ready for cooking, and kept, covered, in the fridge. Tagliatelle tossed with a little grated lemon zest would be a good accompaniment, plus ciabatta with olives or sun-dried tomatoes.

Serves 4

4 skinless boneless chicken breasts (fillets), about 140 g (5 oz) each

100 g (3½ oz) mozzarella cheese, thinly sliced

1 tomato, thinly sliced

1 garlic clove, crushed

1 bunch of fresh basil, about 20 g (¾ oz)

4 slices Parma ham, about 55 g (2 oz) in total

1 tbsp extra virgin olive oil

salt and pepper

Green salad

2 tbsp extra virgin olive oil

juice of ½ lemon

125 g (4½ oz) pack gourmet lettuce selection or mixed salad leaves

1 bunch of watercress, large stalks discarded

Preparation time: 25–30 minutes

Cooking time: about 15 minutes

Each serving provides

kcal 339, **protein** 40 g, **fat** 19 g (of which saturated fat 6 g), **carbohydrate** 1.5 g (of which sugars 1 g), **fibre** 1 g

✓✓✓	B$_6$
✓✓	A, B$_{12}$, C, niacin, calcium, iron
✓	B$_1$, B$_2$, E, folate, copper, potassium, zinc

1 Preheat the oven to 220°C (425°F, gas mark 7). Make a slit along the length of each chicken breast and enlarge to form a pocket.

2 Divide the mozzarella among the chicken breasts, sliding the slices into the pockets. Top the cheese with the tomato slices and crushed garlic. Roughly chop a little of the basil and add a sprinkling to each pocket.

3 Season each chicken breast. Place a large sprig of basil on each, then wrap in a slice of Parma ham, making sure the ham covers the slit in the chicken. Tie the ham securely in place with three or four pieces of string on each breast.

4 Heat the oil in a heavy-based frying pan (preferably one with an ovenproof handle). Add the chicken breasts and fry over a high heat for 3–4 minutes, turning to brown both sides. Transfer the pan to the oven (or transfer the chicken to an oven dish) and bake for 10–12 minutes or until the chicken is cooked through; the juices should run clear when the thickest part of the chicken is pierced with a knife.

5 Meanwhile, make the salad. Put the oil and lemon juice in a bowl, season and mix well together. Add the lettuce and watercress. Toss together, then divide among 4 serving plates.

6 Remove the string from the chicken breasts. Cut each breast across into slices, holding it together so it keeps its shape. Place on the salad and garnish with the remaining basil.

Another idea

• As an alternative to the mozzarella filling, use a mixture of feta cheese and watercress. Soften ½ finely chopped red onion in 15 g (½ oz) butter for 3–5 minutes, then add 75 g (2½ oz) watercress sprigs and cook for a further 1 minute or until the watercress has just wilted. Crumble in 100 g (3½ oz) feta cheese, and season with nutmeg and black pepper.

Plus points

• The Greeks and Romans believed that eating watercress could cure madness. We too attribute healing powers to this green leaf, as it contains powerful phytochemicals that help to protect against cancer. It is also a good source of many B vitamins plus vitamins C, E and beta-carotene, which the body converts into vitamin A.

• Mozzarella contains less fat than many other cheeses. For example, 100 g (3½ oz) mozzarella has 21 g fat and 289 kcal, while the same weight of Cheddar has 34 g fat and 412 kcal.

Turkey kebabs with fennel and red pepper relish

Here lean little bites of turkey are marinated with wine and herbs to add juiciness and flavour, and then threaded onto skewers to be grilled or barbecued. A colourful raw-vegetable relish provides a nice splash of vitamin C as well as a delightful taste contrast. Serve with a complex carbohydrate such as couscous.

Serves 4

450 g (1 lb) skinless turkey breast steak

3 garlic cloves, chopped

1½ tbsp lemon juice

2 tbsp dry white wine

1 tbsp chopped fresh sage or 2 tsp dried sage, crumbled

1 tbsp chopped fresh rosemary

1½ tsp fresh thyme leaves or ½ tsp dried thyme

1 tsp fennel seeds, lightly crushed

2½ tbsp extra virgin olive oil

1 red pepper, seeded and finely diced

1 bulb of fennel, finely diced

1 tbsp black olive paste (tapenade) or 10 black Kalamata olives, finely diced

8 stalks of fresh rosemary (optional)

8 shallots or button onions

salt and pepper

Preparation time: 20 minutes, plus at least 10 minutes marinating

Cooking time: 15 minutes

1 Cut the turkey into 24 pieces, each about 5 x 2 cm (2 x ¾ in). Combine the turkey pieces with 2 of the chopped garlic cloves, 1 tbsp lemon juice, the wine, sage, rosemary, thyme, fennel seeds, 2 tbsp of the olive oil and seasoning. Toss so that all the turkey pieces are covered with the herb mixture. Leave to marinate for at least 10 minutes, or up to 1 hour if you have the time.

2 Meanwhile, make the relish. Put the red pepper, diced fennel and olive paste or diced olives in a bowl together with the remaining garlic, ½ tbsp lemon juice and ½ tbsp olive oil. Season to taste. Mix well, then set aside.

3 Preheat the grill to high, or prepare a charcoal fire in the barbecue. Thread the marinated turkey pieces onto the rosemary stalks if using, or onto skewers, and top each one with a shallot or button onion.

4 Grill or barbecue the kebabs for about 15 minutes or until cooked through and the turkey pieces are lightly browned in spots. Turn the kebabs and baste with the remaining marinade frequently. Serve the kebabs hot, with the red pepper relish.

Plus points

● Red peppers are an excellent source of vitamin C and they are rich in beta-carotene. Both of these nutrients are powerful antioxidants that can help to counteract the damaging effects of free radicals and protect against many diseases including cancer and heart disease.

● Fennel provides useful amounts of potassium and the B vitamin folate. Another of fennel's advantages is that it is low in calories – 100 g (3½ oz) contains 12 kcal.

Each serving provides

kcal 224, **protein** 28 g, **fat** 9.5 g (of which saturated fat 1.5 g), **carbohydrate** 7 g (of which sugars 6 g), **fibre** 2.5 g

✓✓✓	B$_6$, B$_{12}$, C
✓✓	A, niacin
✓	E, folate, copper, iron, potassium, zinc

Some more ideas

• Instead of making a vegetable relish, add the red pepper and fennel to the kebabs. Cut the pepper and fennel into 2.5 cm (1 in) chunks. Alternate the vegetable chunks with pieces of turkey on the skewers, and brush all over with the turkey marinade. Grill or barbecue as above, then serve the turkey and vegetable kebabs drizzled with the remaining extra virgin olive oil and lemon juice.

• Another delicious relish, containing no oil, can be made with roasted red pepper and tomatoes. Cut a large red pepper in half and grill the skin side until it is blistered and charred. Put into a polythene bag and leave until cool enough to handle, then peel off the skin. Finely dice the flesh and mix with 1 diced tomato, 1 finely chopped shallot, 2 chopped garlic cloves, 2 tbsp chopped fresh basil or parsley, a splash of balsamic vinegar, and salt and pepper to taste.

Chicken and yellow pepper loaf

This mustardy chicken and pepper loaf, wrapped in thin slices of courgette instead of high-fat bacon, is perfectly complemented by the fresh tomato and basil sauce – a very colourful dish, full of savoury flavours. Serve the loaf hot with a potato and leek mash, or try it cold with a crunchy raw vegetable salad.

Serves 4

2 tbsp extra virgin olive oil

3 large courgettes, thinly sliced lengthways

2 yellow peppers, seeded and diced

2 bunches of spring onions, thinly sliced

1 garlic clove, crushed

1 tsp mustard powder

500 g (1 lb 2 oz) minced chicken

salt and pepper

Tomato and basil sauce

1 onion, finely chopped

450 g (1 lb) plum tomatoes, coarsely chopped

1 bunch of fresh basil, about 20 g (¾ oz),
   stalks discarded and large leaves torn into
   smaller pieces

pinch of caster sugar

few drops of Tabasco sauce

Preparation time: 40 minutes
Cooking time: 1 hour

Each serving provides

kcal 300, **protein** 29 g, **fat** 14 g (of which saturated fat 3 g), **carbohydrate** 15 g (of which sugars 14 g), **fibre** 5 g

✓✓✓	B$_6$, B$_{12}$, C, folate
✓✓	A, B$_1$, E, niacin, copper, iron, potassium, zinc
✓	B$_2$, calcium, selenium

1 Heat a ridged cast-iron grill pan or griddle, then brush with about 1 tsp of the oil. Grill the courgette slices, in batches, until tender, turning to mark both sides with charred lines. Add a little more oil when necessary. Alternatively, brush the courgette slices with 1 tbsp oil and cook under the grill for 10 minutes, turning once.

2 Meanwhile, heat the remaining 1 tbsp olive oil in a frying pan, add the peppers and cook for 5–6 minutes, stirring frequently, until softened and golden. Add the spring onions and garlic, and cook for a further 2–3 minutes. Sprinkle over the mustard and stir well. Transfer the mixture to a bowl and leave to cool slightly.

3 Add the minced chicken and some seasoning to the bowl and, using your hands, mix well to combine the ingredients thoroughly.

4 Preheat the oven to 180°C (350°F, gas mark 4). Use the courgette slices to line a 900 g (2 lb) loaf tin, laying them crossways and slightly overlapping. Arrange them so the ends hang over the sides of the loaf tin. Spoon the chicken mixture into the tin, pushing the mixture into the corners, and smooth the surface. Fold the ends of the courgette slices over the top of the chicken filling.

5 Set the loaf tin in a roasting tin of water (bain marie). Bake for 1 hour or until the loaf is cooked through; the juices should run clear when a knife is inserted into the centre.

6 About 30 minutes before the end of the cooking time, put all the sauce ingredients in a medium-sized saucepan, reserving a few small basil sprigs for garnish. Bring to a gentle simmer, then cook, stirring occasionally, for 15–20 minutes or until the excess tomato liquid has evaporated. Press the sauce through a sieve into a clean pan, and season to taste. Reheat the sauce.

7 Drain off the juices from the loaf tin, then slice the loaf. Serve hot, with the tomato sauce and garnished with the reserved basil sprigs.

Plus points

- Tomatoes contain lycopene, a carotenoid compound that acts as an antioxidant. Recent studies suggest that lycopene may help to protect against bladder and pancreatic cancers.
- Both the yellow peppers and courgettes provide vitamin C and beta-carotene, which the body converts into vitamin A. The courgettes also contribute folate.

Some more ideas

• Use 1 tbsp Dijon mustard instead of the mustard powder.

• Replace the fresh tomatoes in the sauce with 2 cans chopped tomatoes, 400 g each.

• For a chicken and spinach loaf, line the tin with spinach instead of courgettes. Blanch 200 g (7 oz) large spinach leaves in boiling water just to wilt, then drain and dry on kitchen paper. Brush the tin very lightly with oil. Arrange the spinach leaves over the bottom and sides of the tin, reserving enough to cover the top of the chicken filling. Add another 200 g (7 oz) spinach, cooked, well drained and chopped, to the chicken and pepper mixture.

Sweet and sour chicken pancakes

This is a novel way of serving the popular Chinese dish of stir-fried sweet and sour chicken. Here courgettes and bean sprouts are added, and the mixture is folded up in lacy pancakes.

Serves 4 (makes 8 pancakes)

Pancake batter

115 g (4 oz) plain flour

2 eggs, beaten

200 ml (7 fl oz) semi-skimmed milk

Chicken filling

450 g (1 lb) skinless boneless chicken
   breasts (fillets)

2 tbsp tomato purée

3 tbsp sunflower oil

grated zest and juice of 1 lemon

1 tsp malt vinegar

1 tbsp demerara sugar

2 tsp clear honey

1 onion, halved and sliced

1 courgette, cut into 5 cm (2 in) matchsticks

225 g (8 oz) bean sprouts

1 tsp sesame seeds

2 tbsp rich soy sauce, plus more to serve

salt and pepper

spring onions to garnish

Preparation time: 15 minutes

Cooking time: about 40 minutes

Each serving provides

kcal 445, **protein** 36 g, **fat** 17 g (of which saturated fat 4 g), **carbohydrate** 38 g (of which sugars 14 g), **fibre** 3 g

✓✓✓	B$_6$
✓✓	B$_{12}$, C, E, folate, niacin, copper, iron
✓	A, B$_1$, B$_2$, calcium, potassium, selenium, zinc

1 To make the pancakes, sift the flour into a bowl and season with a little salt and pepper. Make a well in the centre. Mix the eggs, milk and 90 ml (3 fl oz) water together and pour into the well, then whisk in the flour to form a smooth batter. Cover and leave to stand while you prepare the filling.

2 Cut the chicken into long thin strips. Mix together the tomato purée, 1 tbsp of the oil, the lemon zest and juice, vinegar, sugar and honey in a bowl. Add the chicken to this sweet and sour sauce, and toss to coat the strips.

3 Heat a wok or large frying pan and add 1 tbsp of the remaining oil. Add the onion and stir-fry for 5 minutes or until softened. Add the courgette and stir-fry for 3 minutes. Using a draining spoon, remove the vegetables from the wok and set aside.

4 Reheat the wok, then add the chicken mixture and stir-fry for 3–4 minutes or until cooked. Return the vegetables to the wok. Toss together, then remove from the heat and set aside.

5 Heat a 20 cm (8 in) pancake pan, preferably non-stick or well seasoned. Rub a little of the remaining oil over the surface using a crumpled piece of kitchen paper. Pour in a little batter and tilt the pan so that the batter spreads evenly over the surface; tip any excess batter back into the bowl. Cook the pancake over a moderately high heat for 2 minutes, then loosen the edges and flip it over. Cook the second side for about 30 seconds. Slide the pancake onto a plate and cover with a square of greaseproof paper. Repeat with the remaining batter to make 8 pancakes in all, stacking them up, interleaved with greaseproof paper, as they are made. Keep warm over a pan of simmering water, covered with foil.

6 Reheat the filling. Add the bean sprouts, sesame seeds and soy sauce, and stir-fry for 1–2 minutes until everything is hot. Fill the pancakes, fold into quarters and garnish with spring onions. Serve with extra soy sauce.

Plus points

• Bean sprouts, along with other sprouted seeds, are rich in B vitamins and vitamin C. Although some of the vitamin C will be destroyed by cooking, they still contribute good amounts in this recipe.

• Eggs provide valuable amounts of protein and iron. The vitamin C in the bean sprouts, lemon and courgette will help the body to absorb the iron. This mineral is important to prevent anaemia, one of the most common nutritional problems in the UK, particularly among women.

Some more ideas

● Add ½ tsp Chinese five-spice powder to the flour for the pancake batter.

● For chilli chicken pancakes, make the batter as above, adding 1 tsp mild chilli powder to the flour. Omit the sweet and sour sauce mixture. Stir-fry the onion in 1 tbsp sunflower oil with

1 thinly sliced yellow pepper and 100 g (3½ oz) baby sweetcorn, each one cut in half lengthways. Remove the vegetables with a draining spoon and set aside. Add another 1 tbsp oil to the wok and heat, then stir-fry the chicken strips. Return the onion, yellow pepper and sweetcorn to the wok. Add 115 g (4 oz)

finely shredded Chinese leaves, 1 tbsp mild or sweet Chinese chilli sauce and 1½ tsp toasted sesame oil, and toss together for 1–2 minutes. (For more chilli heat in these chilli chicken pancakes, stir-fry 1 fresh red chilli, seeded and cut into very fine strips, with the onion, yellow pepper and sweetcorn.)

Herbed chicken and apple burgers

Adding diced apple – tart or sweet fruit, to your taste – to chicken burgers not only gives a fruity flavour that complements the meat and herbs, but also lightens up the meaty patties and provides fibre. Served in baps or buns, with honey mustard and crisp fresh watercress, these are a great alternative to beefburgers.

Serves 4

340 g (12 oz) minced chicken

1 red onion, finely chopped

4 tbsp fresh breadcrumbs

2 green-skinned apples, such as Granny Smith (for a tart taste) or Golden Delicious (for a sweet taste), coarsely grated

1 tbsp chopped fresh sage

2 tsp fresh thyme leaves

2 tbsp sunflower oil

salt and pepper

To serve

1 tbsp clear honey

3 tbsp Dijon mustard

4 floury baps or burger buns, split open

55 g (2 oz) watercress sprigs, large stalks discarded

Preparation time: 20 minutes, plus 1 hour chilling

Cooking time: 20 minutes

Each serving provides

kcal 430, **protein** 25 g, **fat** 12 g (of which saturated fat 2.5 g), **carbohydrate** 59 g (of which sugars 12 g), **fibre** 3 g

✓✓	B$_6$, B$_{12}$, E, copper, iron, selenium
✓	B$_1$, B$_2$, C, folate, niacin, calcium, potassium, zinc

1 Put the minced chicken, onion, breadcrumbs, apples, herbs and some seasoning in a bowl. Thoroughly mix together with your hands. Wet your hands, then divide the mixture into 4 portions and shape each into a burger. Chill for 1 hour to firm up.

2 Heat the oil in a non-stick frying pan. Add the chicken burgers and cook over a moderate heat until browned on both sides, then reduce the heat a little and continue cooking until the burgers are completely cooked through – about 20 minutes altogether. Turn from time to time to ensure cooking is even.

3 Meanwhile, mix together the honey and mustard. Spread over the top cut surface of each bap or bun. Divide the watercress among the baps, piling it on the bottom cut side.

4 When the chicken burgers have finished cooking, transfer them to the baps, placing them on the watercress. Put on the tops and serve.

Plus points

● Apples provide good amounts of vitamin C as well as soluble fibre in the form of pectin. Eating apples with their skin offers the maximum amount of fibre.

● Minced chicken has much less fat than lean minced beef.

● Each burger offers good amounts of vitamin E (found in the sunflower oil) and selenium (provided by the breadcrumbs) – both powerful antioxidants.

Some more ideas

● Minced turkey will make burgers that are even lower in fat than those made with chicken.

● Use baby spinach leaves instead of watercress.

● For a creamy, more savoury alternative to honey mustard, mix 2 tbsp Dijon mustard with mayonnaise (use reduced-fat mayonnaise, if you prefer).

● Using wholemeal breadcrumbs and wholemeal baps will increase the fibre content.

Turkey sausage and bean hotpot

Healthy eating doesn't mean giving up favourite family meals. Here, lean turkey sausages replace the more traditional pork in a hearty hotpot, with a spicy bean sauce and a covering of thinly sliced root veggies.

Serves 4

400 g (14 oz) potatoes, peeled and thinly sliced

1 large carrot, about 200 g (7 oz), thinly sliced on a diagonal

1 medium parsnip, about 200 g (7 oz), thinly sliced on a diagonal

1½ tbsp sunflower oil

8 turkey sausages, about 450 g (1 lb) in total

1 onion, finely chopped

2 tsp paprika

2 tbsp plain flour

450 ml (15 fl oz) chicken stock, preferably home-made (see page 23)

1 tbsp Worcestershire sauce

3 tsp wholegrain mustard

1 tsp light soft brown sugar

1 can red kidney beans, about 400 g, drained and rinsed

20 g (¾ oz) butter, melted

salt and pepper

Preparation time: about 1 hour
Cooking time: 30–35 minutes

Each serving provides

kcal 486, **protein** 39 g, **fat** 12 g (of which saturated fat 4 g), **carbohydrate** 58 g (of which sugars 15 g), **fibre** 12 g

✓✓✓	A, B$_6$, B$_{12}$
✓✓	B$_1$, E, C, folate, niacin, copper, iron, potassium, zinc
✓	calcium, selenium

1 Preheat the oven to 190°C (375°F, gas mark 5). Cook the potato, carrot and parsnip slices in a saucepan of boiling water for 3–4 minutes or until just tender. Drain and set aside.

2 Heat the oil in a frying pan. Add the sausages and cook over a moderate heat for 10 minutes, turning to brown them evenly. Remove the sausages from the pan and reserve.

3 Add the onion to the pan and sauté for 5 minutes, stirring, until soft and golden. Stir in the paprika and flour, then gradually mix in the stock. Bring to the boil, stirring, then reduce the heat to moderate and simmer until thickened and smooth. Stir in the Worcestershire sauce, 2 tsp of the mustard and the sugar. Season to taste. Add the beans. Cut the sausages into thick slices and stir into the sauce. Bring back to the boil.

4 Spoon the sausage and bean mixture into a 1.5 litre (2¾ pint) shallow baking dish. Arrange the sliced root vegetables over the top, starting in the centre and working out in overlapping rings to cover the surface completely. Mix the remaining 1 tsp of mustard with the melted butter and brush over the vegetables.

5 Bake for 30–35 minutes or until the sauce is bubbling and the vegetable topping is golden brown. Serve hot.

Some more ideas

• The hotpot can be prepared in advance and kept in the fridge until ready to bake. Allow 40–45 minutes cooking time, covering the top of the dish with foil after 20 minutes.

• For a vegetarian version, use meat-free sausages and vegetable stock. Replace the Worcestershire sauce with mild chilli sauce.

• Use 2 sliced leeks, about 250 g (9 oz) in total, instead of onion, and omit the paprika. Use cannellini beans, and add 55 g (2 oz) ready-to-eat pitted prunes, halved.

• Instead of the sliced vegetable topping, make a mash: cut the potatoes, carrot and parsnip into chunks and cook in boiling water for 15–20 minutes or until very tender. Drain well, then mash with 200 g (7 oz) fromage frais – virtually fat-free, if you prefer – and season to taste. Spread over the sausage and bean mixture, then dot with 15 g (½ oz) butter and sprinkle with a little paprika. Bake as above.

Plus points

• Red kidney beans – and all other pulses – are a good source of dietary fibre, particularly soluble fibre which can help to reduce high blood cholesterol levels.

• Both parsnips and potatoes provide useful amounts of potassium. Parsnips also contain useful quantities of some of the B vitamins, particularly folate and B$_1$.

Chicken fajitas with tomato salsa

Although in northern Mexico 'fajitas' refers to a specific cut of beef, elsewhere in the world the term has come to describe a combination of sizzling pan-grilled chicken strips with peppers and onions, wrapped in a flour tortilla. The dish has very little fat, but lots and lots of fresh flavours.

Serves 4

400 g (14 oz) skinless boneless chicken breasts (fillets), cut into strips

2 garlic cloves, chopped

1 tsp ground cumin

1 tsp mild chilli powder

1 tsp paprika

¼ tsp dried oregano

grated zest and juice of ½ orange

juice of ½ lemon

2 tbsp sunflower oil

30 g (1 oz) fresh coriander leaves, chopped

2 green peppers, seeded and thinly sliced lengthways

2 onions, thinly sliced lengthways

8 flour tortillas

120 ml (4 fl oz) soured cream

salt and pepper

sprigs of fresh coriander to garnish

Tomato salsa

4 spring onions, thinly sliced

125 g (4½ oz) ripe tomatoes, diced

1 medium-hot fresh green chilli, seeded and chopped, or to taste

2 tbsp tomato passata

2 garlic cloves, chopped

½ tsp ground cumin

lemon juice to taste

Preparation time: 30 minutes

Cooking time: 25–30 minutes

1 In a bowl combine the chicken strips with the garlic, cumin, chilli, paprika, oregano, orange zest and juice, lemon juice, 1 tbsp of the oil and 3 tbsp of the coriander. Mix well so that all the chicken strips are coated, then leave to marinate for at least 15 minutes, or while you prepare the rest of the dish.

2 To make the salsa, combine all the ingredients. Add the remaining chopped coriander. Season with ¼–½ tsp lemon juice and some salt and pepper to taste. Set aside.

3 Preheat the oven to 180°C (350°F, gas mark 4) and preheat the grill to high. Heat a ridged cast-iron grill pan or heavy-based frying pan until it is very hot. Brush with the remaining 1 tbsp of oil. Put in the green peppers and onions and cook for 6–8 minutes or until tender and lightly charred (do this in batches, if necessary). Remove from the pan and set aside.

4 Wrap the tortillas, stacked up, in foil and put into the oven to warm for 10 minutes. Meanwhile, spread out the chicken in a shallow layer in the grill pan. Grill close to the heat, turning once or twice, for about 5 minutes or until thoroughly cooked.

5 To serve, divide the chicken, onions and peppers among the warm tortillas and roll up. Garnish with sprigs of coriander and serve with the fresh salsa and soured cream. Alternatively, present the ingredients separately, with the tortillas wrapped in a cloth to keep them warm, and let your guests make their own fajitas.

Plus points

• Onions and garlic are not just valuable assets in the kitchen, they have been used throughout history as a cure-all. Recent research suggests that they can help to lower blood cholesterol and so reduce the risk of heart disease. They also prevent blood clotting and are a natural decongestant. So include onions and garlic in your cooking as much as possible.

• The vitamin C in the fresh salsa helps the body to absorb the iron from the chicken.

Each serving provides

kcal 495, **protein** 29 g, **fat** 17 g (of which saturated fat 6 g), **carbohydrate** 60 g (of which sugars 10 g), **fibre** 5 g

✓✓✓	B_6, C
✓✓	E, niacin, copper, iron
✓	A, B_1, B_2, folate, calcium, potassium, selenium, zinc

Some more ideas

• The chicken can be stir-fried in a hot wok or non-stick frying pan, or can be cooked on the grill pan, instead of grilling. You could also cook these fajitas on a barbecue, threaded onto metal skewers so that they do not fall into the fire.

• For quesadillas, use only 170 g (6 oz) chicken. Allow 4 flour tortillas (1 per person) for the recipe rather than 8 (2 each). Sprinkle one half of each tortilla with 30 g (1 oz) grated cheese such as Cheddar and add a spoonful or two of the hot cooked chicken strips and the hot green peppers and onions. Fold over into a half-moon shape, pressing the edges together, and cook in a hot frying pan until the tortilla is very lightly golden on each side and the cheese has melted. Serve each quesadilla with a dollop of salsa (omit the soured cream).

Super Sandwiches

Delicious snacks to keep you on the go

Whatever your taste in snacks and light meals, you'll find something to tempt you here. There are spiced strips of chicken grilled and stuffed into pitta bread with salad and tzatziki; hot turkey and melted Stilton on bagel halves; roasted chicken thighs with a mustard and honey glaze served in baps with luscious mango. For an Indian-style snack try a mix of chicken, broccoli and cashews rolled up in chapattis. Or you might enjoy Italian-style pasties made with chicken, sun-dried tomatoes, olives and roasted peppers baked in pizza dough. Or picnic in style with a whole hollowed-out loaf packed with turkey, pesto sauce, avocado, tomatoes and crisp peppery greens.

Greek chicken pittas

These chicken pittas are packed with tasty salad leaves and the Greek cucumber and yogurt sauce called tzatziki. They are incredibly quick and easy to prepare, so when you are next short of time, don't reach for the take-away menu – put together some delicious, healthy chicken pittas instead.

Serves 4

550 g (1¼ lb) skinless boneless chicken
   breasts (fillets)
4 tbsp instant polenta
½ tsp dried onion granules
1 tsp paprika
1 tsp cumin seeds
1 tsp coarsely ground black pepper
½ tsp salt
2 tbsp extra virgin olive oil
4 pitta breads
115 g (4 oz) mixed herb salad leaves

Tzatziki

7.5 cm (3 in) piece cucumber, grated
100 g (3½ oz) Greek-style yogurt
100 g (3½ oz) plain low-fat yogurt
1 large garlic clove, crushed
1 tsp mint sauce
1 tbsp chopped fresh mint

Preparation time: 15 minutes
Cooking time: about 8 minutes

1 Cut the chicken breasts into thin strips. Mix together the polenta, onion granules, paprika, cumin seeds, pepper and salt in a polythene bag. Add the chicken strips, a few at a time, and toss well to coat all over. Remove, shaking off the excess, and set aside on a plate while making the tzatziki.

2 Squeeze the grated cucumber, in handfuls, to remove excess moisture, then put into a bowl. Add the remaining ingredients and stir to mix. Set aside.

3 Preheat the grill. Heat a griddle or heavy-based frying pan and add half the oil, swirling it round the pan until lightly coated. Add half the chicken strips and cook over a high heat for 2–3 minutes or until golden brown all over and cooked through, turning once. Keep hot while cooking the remaining chicken strips, using the rest of the oil.

4 Meanwhile, warm the pitta breads under the grill for 1 minute on each side. Split down the side of each pitta to make a pocket.

5 Fill the pitta pockets with the salad leaves. Pile in the chicken strips, spoon over the tzatziki and serve.

Plus points

● Yogurt is a good source of calcium and, generally, low in fat. Traditional Greek-style yogurt is higher in fat than plain low-fat yogurt (1.35 g fat per level tbsp as compared to 0.12 g), but mixing the two together means you reduce the total amount of fat while retaining the creaminess that Greek yogurt gives. Look out for 'lite' Greek-style yogurt, which still has all the properties of traditional Greek yogurt with only 0.75 g fat per tbsp.

● Always serve snack foods with plenty of fresh salads and vegetables. Even a spoonful of chopped parsley will increase the iron and vitamin C content of the meal.

Each serving provides

kcal 555, **protein** 44 g, **fat** 13 g (of which saturated fat 3 g), **carbohydrate** 69 g (of which sugars 5 g), **fibre** 3 g

✓✓	B₁, B₂, B₆, niacin, calcium, iron, potassium, selenium, zinc
✓	folate, copper

super sandwiches

140

Some more ideas

- Use wholemeal pitta for extra fibre.
- If you cannot find dried onion granules, use onion salt and omit the ½ tsp salt.
- For a hot Middle Eastern-style sandwich, put the whole chicken breasts between sheets of cling film and bat out with a rolling pin to a thickness of about 1 cm (½ in) all over. Lightly beat 1 egg and pour onto a plate. Put 100 g (3½ oz) fine fresh white breadcrumbs on another plate. Season each chicken escalope, then dip into the egg and coat both sides in breadcrumbs, patting them on lightly. Heat half the oil in a griddle or frying pan and add 2 of the chicken breasts. Cook for 6 minutes, turning once, until golden. Keep hot while cooking the other 2 chicken breasts. Meanwhile, finely shred 100 g (3½ oz) each white and red cabbage, and thinly slice 75 g (2½ oz) sweet white onion such as Vidalia. Toss with 2 tbsp chopped parsley and 2 tbsp lemon juice. Spoon 1 tbsp hummus into each warmed pitta pocket, add some cabbage salad and fill with the hot chicken escalopes.

Hot turkey and Stilton bagels

Favourite Christmas flavours make this a most glamorous toasted open-face sandwich. If you keep a supply of bagels in the freezer, you can rustle up a great snack meal like this whenever you have some leftover turkey or chicken. Serve with a mixed fruit and vegetable salad.

Serves 4

4 bagels, plain or onion-flavoured

30 g (1 oz) butter

2 tbsp cranberry jelly

225 g (8 oz) cold roast turkey meat, skin removed, then thinly sliced

100 g (3½ oz) Stilton cheese

To serve

2 oranges, cut into wedges

salad leaves

Preparation time: 10 minutes

Cooking time: 5 minutes

1 Preheat the grill. Split the bagels in half horizontally, then toast both sides under the grill.

2 Spread the cut surfaces of the bagel halves lightly with butter, then spread over the cranberry jelly. Arrange the sliced turkey on the bagel halves.

3 Slice or crumble the Stilton cheese and place on top of the turkey. Return to the grill to cook for 1–2 minutes, just to melt the cheese.

4 Serve hot, with the orange wedges and salad leaves.

Some more ideas

● Instead of bagels, use muffins or ciabatta rolls split in half.

● Cooked chicken could be substituted for the roast turkey.

● Blue Vinney is a lower-fat alternative to Stilton. If you're not fond of blue cheese, use thinly sliced Gruyère or Camembert, or even a well-flavoured Cheddar, coarsely grated; sliced Gouda will reduce the fat.

● For another hot turkey sandwich, toast 8 thick slices of brioche loaf, or split brioche buns, on both sides and butter very lightly. Warm 120 ml (4 fl oz) leftover turkey gravy (or make a sauce from 4 tbsp each red wine and stock, thickened with 2 tsp cornflour mixed with a little water). Add the sliced turkey to the hot gravy or sauce and heat through, then spoon on top of the toasted brioche. Top each slice with 1 tsp cranberry or redcurrant jelly, garnish with watercress and serve.

Plus points

● Although Stilton is relatively high in fat, it has a strong flavour so a little goes a long way. Like all cheese, it is a good source of protein and a valuable source of calcium, phosphorus, and the B vitamins B_{12} and niacin.

● Bread is an important part of a healthy diet, as it is a complex carbohydrate, and also contributes fibre, vitamins and minerals, particularly calcium.

Each serving provides

kcal 435, **protein** 28 g, **fat** 17 g (of which saturated fat 10 g), **carbohydrate** 40 g (of which sugars 17 g), **fibre** 2.5 g

✓✓✓	B_{12}, C
✓✓	folate
✓	A, B_6, niacin, calcium, copper, zinc

super sandwiches

Sweet roasted chicken bap

Few snacks can be more universally popular than sandwiches. The possibilities for healthy fillings are endless, although fat and calories can climb when dressings are added. Try this sweet and spicy combination of lean chicken roasted with a honey and mustard dressing, juicy mango slices and crisp lettuce leaves.

Serves 4

6 tbsp wholegrain mustard

4 tsp clear honey

4 skinless boneless chicken thighs, about 85 g (3 oz) each

4 large baps, plain or wholemeal

8 small Cos lettuce leaves

2 small ripe mangoes, sliced

2 spring onions, thinly sliced (optional)

salt and pepper

Preparation time: 10 minutes

Cooking time: 12–15 minutes

1 Preheat the oven to 180°C (350°F, gas mark 4). Mix the mustard and honey together and season to taste.

2 Enlarge the hollow left by the bone in each chicken thigh, cutting to open them out. Press to flatten them a little. Place the thighs, smooth side up, in a lightly oiled ovenproof dish or small roasting tin. Set aside about 2 tbsp of the honey and mustard mixture, and spread the remainder over the top of the chicken thighs. Roast for 12–15 minutes or until the juices run clear when a thigh is pierced with a knife.

3 Meanwhile, split open the baps and toast them. Place a lettuce leaf on the bottom half of each bap, top with the mango slices and sprinkle with the spring onions, if using. Spread the reserved honey and mustard mixture over the underside of the top halves.

4 Put the roasted chicken thighs on top of the mango and spring onions, then top with the remaining lettuce. Put the tops of the baps on and press the sandwiches gently together. Serve immediately.

Some more ideas

• You can roast the chicken in advance and serve it chilled, rather than hot.

• To make an open-face sandwich, place the lettuce, mango slices and chicken thighs on toasted thick slices of country-style bread.

• Use turkey breast fillets instead of chicken thighs. Because they are a denser meat they cook more quickly – roast for 10–12 minutes.

• Ring the changes with the fruit you use – try slices of fresh pineapple, peach or kiwi. If you use canned fruits, select ones canned in fruit juice rather than syrup, to keep the calorie count low.

• For a chicken and vegetable sandwich, top the roasted mustard-glazed chicken with the grated courgette, carrot and sweet onion salad on page 59, or serve with a carrot and white cabbage coleslaw.

• Wholegrain mustard adds texture to the sandwich, but if you prefer you can substitute a smooth German-style mustard.

Plus points

• Wholegrain mustard, which includes oil, has 10.2 g fat and 140 kcal per 100 g (3½ oz), but this is significantly less than mayonnaise, which contains a whopping 75.6 g fat and 691 kcal for the same amount.

Each serving provides

kcal 365, **protein** 25 g, **fat** 9 g (of which saturated fat 2 g), **carbohydrate** 49 g (of which sugars 19 g), **fibre** 7 g

✓✓✓ C

✓✓ A, B_6, B_{12}, niacin, copper, iron, selenium, zinc

✓ B_1, B_2, E, folate, calcium, potassium

Chicken and broccoli chapatti

These mouth-watering Indian-style snacks are very quick to make. Chapattis are the healthiest of Indian breads, as they are often made with wholemeal flour and are usually cooked on a dry griddle or pan without any fat. A yogurt-based raita, containing cucumber and tomato, is the perfect accompaniment.

Serves 4

200 g (7 oz) cooked chicken meat

2 tbsp sunflower oil

250 g (9 oz) broccoli florets, finely chopped

45 g (1½ oz) unsalted cashew nuts, coarsely chopped

2 tsp grated fresh root ginger

1 garlic clove, finely chopped

4 tbsp mango chutney

4 chapattis

pepper

To serve

Raita (see page 80)

Preparation time: about 10 minutes
Cooking time: about 10 minutes

Each serving provides

kcal 326, protein 21 g, fat 16 g (of which saturated fat 3 g), carbohydrate 35 g (of which sugars 10 g), fibre 2 g

✓✓✓	C
✓✓	B₆, E, folate, copper, iron
✓	B₁, niacin, calcium, potassium, zinc

1 Preheat the grill. Cut the chicken into small bite-sized pieces, discarding any skin.

2 Heat the oil in a large frying pan, add the broccoli, cashews, ginger and garlic, and cook for 5 minutes, stirring, until the broccoli is tender.

3 Add the chicken, mango chutney and pepper to taste to the broccoli mixture and stir to mix. Cook for a further 2 minutes, stirring constantly, until the chicken is hot.

4 Meanwhile, place the chapattis on the rack in the grill pan and sprinkle with water. Grill for 2 minutes, turning once.

5 Put the chicken mixture on top of the chapattis and roll them up. Serve hot, with a raita accompaniment.

Some more ideas

● Cauliflower florets can be used as an alternative to the broccoli.

● For a snack with Mexican flavours, use 8 flour tortillas instead of chapattis. Heat the tortillas, one at a time, in a dry frying pan for 20 seconds, turning once. Make a quick fresh tomato salsa by mixing together 4 ripe tomatoes, skinned and finely diced, 1 small onion, finely chopped, 1–2 tbsp finely chopped fresh coriander, a squeeze of lemon or lime juice, a few drops of Tabasco sauce, and pepper to taste. Prepare the chicken and broccoli mixture as above, omitting the ginger and mango chutney, and using pine nuts instead of cashews. Divide the chicken mixture among the hot flour tortillas, add a spoonful of tomato salsa to each and roll up.

Plus points

● Broccoli is packed with vitamins. It is an excellent source of the antioxidants beta-carotene and vitamin C as well as vitamin E. It also provides good amounts of the B vitamins niacin and B₆ and useful amounts of folate. Just 1 serving of cooked broccoli (about 85 g/3 oz) would provide nearly 50% of the recommended daily intake of vitamin C.

● In common with other members of the Cruciferae family of vegetables, such as cauliflower, Brussels sprouts, cabbage and kale, broccoli contains a number of different phytochemicals. One of these, indoles, may help to protect against breast cancer by inhibiting the action of the oestrogens that trigger the growth of tumours.

Mexican tostadas

Tostadas comes from the Spanish word for toasted – in Mexico it refers to flat, crisply toasted corn tortillas, topped with all sorts of savoury things. Chicken with beans and salad is a favourite. A base layer of a thick mixture – often refried beans, but here a spicy pepper and tomato mixture – keeps everything together.

Serves 4

2 chicken breasts, about 500 g (1 lb 2 oz) in total, skinned

2 tbsp extra virgin olive oil

2 red peppers, seeded and coarsely chopped

1 onion, coarsely chopped

2 garlic cloves, thinly sliced

1 tbsp mild chilli powder

2 tsp paprika

1 tsp ground cumin

1 can chopped tomatoes, about 400 g

pinch of sugar

8 corn tortillas

1 can borlotti or pinto beans, about 425 g

salt and pepper

To serve

1 tomato, diced

pickled jalapeño chillies (optional)

125 g (4½ oz) iceberg lettuce, shredded

8 radishes, sliced

4 tbsp soured cream

Tabasco or other hot chilli sauce

Preparation time: 35 minutes
Cooking time: 20 minutes

1 Place the chicken in a saucepan with cold water to cover. Bring to the boil, then reduce the heat and simmer for 10–15 minutes. Remove from the heat and leave to cool in the liquid. When cool enough to handle, drain and take the meat from the bones. Shred the meat and set aside.

2 Heat the olive oil in a frying pan and add the peppers, onion and garlic. Sauté over a moderate heat for 5 minutes or until softened. Add the chilli powder, paprika and cumin, stir well, and cook for a few more minutes. Stir in the tomatoes with their juice and the sugar. Simmer for 5–8 minutes or until thick. Season to taste. Remove from the heat and keep warm.

3 Heat a heavy-based frying pan. Toast the tortillas, one at a time, for about 15 seconds on each side or until slightly crisp and lightly browned. As they are done, keep them warm stacked in a tea towel. Meanwhile, warm the beans in the can liquid. Drain well.

4 Place 2 toasted tortillas on each plate. Spread with the tomato mixture, then spoon on the beans and chicken. Add diced tomato, pickled jalapeños, if using, lettuce and radishes, piling up these toppings. Finish with a spoonful of soured cream. Serve with Tabasco sauce to be added to taste.

Another idea

● Instead of beans, use a mixture of sweetcorn and courgette. Cook 1 corn on the cob and 1 whole courgette in separate pans of boiling water until tender, about 5 minutes for the corn and 10 minutes for the courgette. Drain. Dice the courgette, and cut the kernels of corn off the cob. Scatter the vegetables over each sauce-spread tortilla, then add the chicken.

Plus points

● Pulses such as borlotti and pinto beans are a good source of soluble fibre and an excellent source of protein – even better when they are eaten with grains such as wheat or maize (in corn tortillas).

● Radishes are low in fat and calories, and provide useful amounts of vitamin C. They contain phytochemicals that may help to protect against cancer.

Each serving provides

kcal 425, **protein** 31 g, **fat** 11 g (of which saturated fat 3 g), **carbohydrate** 53 g (of which sugars 14 g), **fibre** 10 g

✓✓✓	A, C, B$_6$, niacin
✓✓	B$_1$, E, folate, calcium, iron, potassium, selenium
✓	B$_2$, copper, zinc

Calzone with roasted peppers

Calzone is a bit like an Italian version of a Cornish pasty, but with the tasty filling sealed inside pizza dough rather than pastry. This recipe combines diced chicken with olives, roasted peppers, fresh basil and mozzarella cheese to make an ideal snack for a packed lunch or picnic.

Serves 4

2 red peppers, halved and seeded
1 tbsp extra virgin olive oil
1 large onion, sliced
3 garlic cloves, crushed
300 g (10½ oz) skinless boneless chicken
    breasts (fillets), diced
12 sun-dried tomato halves packed in oil,
    drained and chopped
4 tbsp chopped fresh basil
12 stoned black olives, halved
1 packet pizza base mix, about 290 g
150 g (5½ oz) mozzarella cheese, diced
1 egg, beaten
1 tbsp sesame seeds
salt and pepper

Preparation time: 50 minutes, plus 15 minutes
    rising
Cooking time: 15 minutes

Each serving provides

kcal 610, **protein** 36 g, **fat** 24 g (of which
saturated fat 8 g), **carbohydrate** 65 g (of
which sugars 9 g), **fibre** 4.5 g

✓✓✓	A, B$_6$, B$_{12}$, C, calcium
✓✓	B$_1$, E, niacin, copper, iron
✓	B$_2$, folate, potassium, zinc

1 Preheat the oven to 220°C (425°F, gas mark 7) and lightly oil a baking tray. Place the peppers on the tray, cut side down, and roast for 10–15 minutes or until the skins are wrinkled and are starting to char. When the peppers have finished roasting, put them in a polythene bag and leave until cool enough to handle. Leave the oven on.

2 Meanwhile, heat the oil in a frying pan, add the onion and garlic, and fry over a moderately low heat, stirring frequently, for 10 minutes or until softened and starting to turn golden.

3 Add the chicken to the pan and fry for 2 more minutes or until the chicken changes colour (it will not be cooked through). Remove from the heat. Stir in the sun-dried tomatoes, basil, olives and seasoning. Set aside.

4 Make up the pizza dough – using both sachets – with 240 ml (8 fl oz) tepid water, or according to packet instructions. Knead the dough briefly until smooth, then cut it into 4 portions. Roll out each piece on a lightly floured work surface to a 20 cm (8 in) round.

5 Peel the skins from the roasted peppers, then roughly chop the flesh. Stir the peppers and mozzarella into the chicken mixture. Pile one-quarter of the chicken filling in the centre of each dough round.

6 Brush the edge of each dough round with beaten egg, then fold over into a half-moon. Seal the edges by firmly folding them over and crimping together. Place the calzone on a lightly oiled baking tray and cover loosely with cling film. Leave to rise in a warm place for 15 minutes.

7 Uncover the calzone and brush with beaten egg. Sprinkle with the sesame seeds. Bake for 15 minutes or until golden brown. Serve warm or at room temperature.

Another idea

● For Spanish empanadas, use yellow peppers instead of red; dice them and soften with the onion and garlic rather than roasting them. Use 1 tsp fresh thyme leaves instead of the basil, 1 tbsp sweet chilli sauce instead of the sun-dried tomatoes, and green olives instead of black. Omit the mozzarella and instead add 100 g (3½ oz) skinned and chopped chorizo sausage to the pan with the chicken, and 2 tbsp currants.

Plus points

● Red peppers are an excellent source of vitamin C. Even when roasted, useful amounts of the vitamin remain.

super sandwiches

Avocado chicken club sandwich

In true American style, this club sandwich is piled high, and packs in lots of interesting flavours and textures. Parma ham, fried until crisp, replaces the usual bacon, and mashed avocado the butter. Adding a few leaves to a sandwich is a cunning way to get children to eat their greens.

Serves 4

12 slices mixed grain bread

4 tbsp mayonnaise

115 g (4 oz) iceberg lettuce, finely shredded

115 g (4 oz) cooked chicken breast meat, skin removed, then sliced

4 slices Parma ham, cut into strips

1 avocado

1 tbsp lime juice

1 orange, peeled and chopped

1 bunch of watercress, tough stalks discarded

20 g (¾ oz) alfalfa sprouts

2 tsp pumpkin seeds, toasted

pepper

Preparation time: about 20 minutes

1 Spread 4 slices of bread with half of the mayonnaise. Divide the shredded lettuce among the slices, then add the sliced chicken breast.

2 Heat a non-stick pan and dry fry the strips of Parma ham for 1–2 minutes or until crisp and curly. Pile on top of the chicken and season with pepper (the ham is salty). Spread mayonnaise on another 4 slices of bread and put these, mayonnaise-side down, on the chicken and ham.

3 Mash the avocado flesh with the lime juice. Divide among the sandwiches, spooning onto the bread and spreading out roughly. Top with the chopped orange, watercress, alfalfa sprouts and pumpkin seeds. Put the final slices of bread on top. Press down gently, then cut each sandwich in half or into quarters for serving.

Some more ideas

● Use mustard and cress if alfalfa sprouts are not available.

● Use reduced-fat mayonnaise to cut down on the fat even more.

● Replace the orange with dry-pack sun-dried tomatoes, rehydrated in water and then finely chopped.

● Substitute chopped chicory leaves for the watercress.

● For fruity chicken club sandwiches, replace the top deck of avocado, orange, watercress, alfalfa sprouts and pumpkin seeds on each sandwich with 1 tbsp crunchy peanut butter, ½ sliced banana sprinkled with a little lemon juice, 2 fresh dates, skinned and chopped, and 1 tsp chopped parsley.

Plus points

● Avocados have a reputation for being a 'fatty' fruit, but most of their fat is of the good, unsaturated type, making them a valuable source of essential fatty acids as well as vitamin E.

● Pumpkin seeds contain a variety of useful minerals, including phosphorus, magnesium and copper, as well as fibre and protein. Pumpkin seeds are also a rich source of fat, as are sunflower and other seeds, but this is mostly the healthy, unsaturated type.

Each serving provides

kcal 535, **protein** 24 g, **fat** 24 g (of which saturated fat 4 g), **carbohydrate** 58 g (of which sugars 7 g), **fibre** 8 g

✓✓✓	C
✓✓	B_1, B_6, E, folate, niacin, calcium, copper, iron, zinc
✓	A, B_1, potassium

super sandwiches

Provençal turkey sandwich

Around the Mediterranean, a 'sandwich' of cold meat and salad vegetables packed into a hollowed-out bread loaf was traditionally carried into the fields by workers, to provide a protein-packed carbohydrate-rich snack at lunchtime. This up-to-date version uses low-fat turkey, moistened with fragrant basil pesto.

Serves 4

1 rustic crusty loaf, about 400 g (14 oz)

3 tbsp pesto sauce

1 large beefsteak tomato, about 200 g (7 oz), sliced

55 g (2 oz) mixed rocket and watercress

1 avocado, sliced

1 tbsp lemon juice

170 g (6 oz) cooked turkey meat, skin removed, then thickly sliced

salt and pepper

Preparation time: 15 minutes, plus at least 1 hour chilling

1 Slice a 'lid' from the top of the loaf. Remove the soft bread from the underside of the lid and from the centre of the loaf, to leave a 2 cm (¾ in) thick lid and shell. Spread the pesto evenly over the underside of the lid and all over the inside of the bread shell.

2 Arrange half of the sliced tomato round the bottom of the shell and season to taste. Add half the rocket and watercress, scattering it evenly over the tomatoes. Sprinkle the sliced avocado with the lemon juice, then arrange in a layer over the greens. Next add the sliced turkey and season to taste. Arrange the remaining tomato slices on top and finish with the remaining rocket and watercress. Press the filling down gently and replace the lid.

3 Wrap the loaf in foil or cling film and refrigerate for at least 1 hour or until ready to serve. Cut the loaf into quarters for serving.

Some more ideas

● Make individual sandwiches with 4 large ciabatta rolls or other crusty rolls.

● Instead of pesto use black olive paste (tapenade) or sun-dried tomato paste.

● Make a vegetarian version by replacing the turkey with aubergine. Cut 1 aubergine into 8 thick slices, brush them lightly with extra virgin olive oil, and grill until tender and lightly browned on both sides. Use 1 thinly sliced red pepper instead of the avocado.

Plus points

● The health benefits of eating watercress have been acknowledged for many centuries. Hippocrates wrote about its medicinal value in 460 BC, and built the world's first hospital next to a stream so he could grow fresh watercress for his patients. Watercress provides good amounts of several antioxidants, including vitamin C, vitamin E and carotenoid compounds, and substantial amounts of the B vitamins folate, niacin and B_6.

● The positive aspects of eating bread were long unappreciated because it was thought to be fattening – which is not true. In fact, even white bread provides useful amounts of fibre, and by law it is fortified with vitamins and calcium.

Each serving provides

kcal 400, **protein** 23 g, **fat** 13 g (of which saturated fat 3 g), **carbohydrate** 50 g (of which sugars 3 g), **fibre** 3 g

✓✓	B_6, niacin, selenium
✓	B_{12}, E, folate, calcium, copper, iron, potassium, zinc

super sandwiches

A glossary of nutritional terms

Antioxidants These are compounds that help to protect the body's cells against the damaging effects of free radicals. Vitamins C and E, beta-carotene (the plant form of vitamin A) and the mineral selenium, together with many of the phytochemicals found in fruit and vegetables, all act as antioxidants.

Calorie A unit used to measure the energy value of food and the intake and use of energy by the body. The scientific definition of 1 calorie is the amount of heat required to raise the temperature of 1 gram of water by 1 degree Centigrade. This is such a small amount that in this country we tend to use the term kilocalories (abbreviated to *kcal*), which is equivalent to 1000 calories. Energy values can also be measured in kilojoules (kJ): 1 kcal = 4.2 kJ.

A person's energy (calorie) requirement varies depending on his or her age, sex and level of activity. The estimated average daily energy requirements are:

Age (years)	Female (kcal)	Male (kcal)
1–3	1165	1230
4–6	1545	1715
7–10	1740	1970
11–14	1845	2220
15–18	2110	2755
19–49	1940	2550
50–59	1900	2550
60–64	1900	2380
65–74	1900	2330

Carbohydrates These energy-providing substances are present in varying amounts in different foods and are found in three main forms: sugars, starches and non-starch polysaccharides (NSP), usually called fibre.

There are two types of sugars: *intrinsic sugars*, which occur naturally in fruit (fructose) and sweet-tasting vegetables, and *extrinsic sugars*, which include lactose (from milk) and all the non-milk extrinsic sugars (NMEs) – sucrose (table sugar), honey, treacle, molasses and so on. The NMEs, or 'added' sugars, provide only calories, whereas foods containing intrinsic sugars also offer vitamins, minerals and fibre. Added sugars (*simple carbohydrates*) are digested and absorbed rapidly to provide energy very quickly. Starches and fibre (*complex carbohydrates*), on the other hand, break down more slowly to offer a longer-term energy source (see also Glycaemic Index). Starchy carbohydrates are found in bread, pasta, rice, wholegrain and breakfast cereals, and potatoes and other starchy vegetables such as parsnips, sweet potatoes and yams.

Healthy eating guidelines recommend that at least half of our daily energy (calories) should come from carbohydrates, and that most of this should be from complex carbohydrates. No more than 11% of our total calorie intake should come from 'added' sugars. For an average woman aged 19–49 years, this would mean a total carbohydrate intake of 259 g per day, of which 202 g should be from starch and intrinsic sugars and no more than 57 g from added sugars. For a man of the same age, total carbohydrates each day should be about 340 g (265 g from starch and intrinsic sugars and 75 g from added sugars).

See also Fibre and Glycogen.

Cholesterol There are two types of cholesterol – the soft waxy substance called blood cholesterol, which is an integral part of human cell membranes, and dietary cholesterol, which is contained in food. *Blood cholesterol* is important in the formation of some hormones and it aids digestion. High blood cholesterol levels are known to be an important risk factor for coronary heart disease, but most of the cholesterol in our blood is made by the liver – only about 25% comes from cholesterol in food. So while it would seem that the amount of cholesterol-rich foods in the diet would have a direct effect on blood cholesterol levels, in fact the best way to reduce blood cholesterol is to eat less saturated fat and to increase intake of foods containing soluble fibre.

Fat Although a small amount of fat is essential for good health, most people consume far too much. Healthy eating guidelines recommend that no more than 33% of our daily energy intake (calories) should come from fat. Each gram of fat contains 9 kcal, more than twice as many calories as carbohydrate or protein, so for a woman aged 19–49 years this means a daily maximum of 71 g fat, and for a man in the same age range 93.5 g fat.

Fats can be divided into 3 main groups: saturated, monounsaturated and polyunsaturated, depending on the chemical structure of the fatty acids they contain. *Saturated fatty acids* are found mainly in animal fats such as butter and other dairy products and in fatty meat. A high intake of saturated fat is known to be a risk factor for coronary heart disease and certain types of cancer. Current guidelines are that no more than 10% of our daily calories should come from saturated fats, which is about 21.5 g for an adult woman and 28.5 g for a man.

Where saturated fats tend to be solid at room temperature, the *unsaturated fatty acids* – monounsaturated and polyunsaturated – tend to be liquid. *Monounsaturated fats* are found predominantly in olive oil, groundnut (peanut) oil, rapeseed oil and avocados. Foods high in *polyunsaturates* include most vegetable oils – the exceptions are palm oil and coconut oil, both of which are saturated.

Both saturated and monounsaturated fatty acids can be made by the body, but certain polyunsaturated fatty acids – known as *essential fatty acids* – must be supplied by food. There are 2 'families' of these essential fatty acids: *omega-6*, derived from linoleic acid, and *omega-3*, from linolenic acid. The main food sources of the omega-6 family are vegetable oils such as olive and sunflower; omega-3 fatty acids are provided by oily fish, nuts, and vegetable oils such as soya and rapeseed.

When vegetable oils are hydrogenated (hardened) to make margarine and reduced-fat spreads, their unsaturated fatty acids can be changed into trans fatty acids, or '*trans fats*'. These artificially produced trans fats are believed to act in the same way as saturated fats within the body – with the same risks to health. Current healthy eating guidelines suggest that no more than 2% of our daily calories should come from trans fats, which is about 4.3 g for an adult woman and 5.6 g for a man. In thinking about the amount of trans fats you consume, remember that major sources are processed foods such as biscuits, pies, cakes and crisps.

Fibre Technically non-starch polysaccharides (NSP), fibre is the term commonly used to describe several different compounds, such as pectin, hemicellulose, lignin and gums, which are found in the cell walls of all plants. The body cannot digest fibre, nor does it have much nutritional value, but it plays an important role in helping us to stay healthy.

Fibre can be divided into 2 groups – soluble and insoluble. Both types are provided by most plant foods, but some foods are particularly good sources of one type or the other. *Soluble fibre* (in oats, pulses, fruit and vegetables) can help to reduce high blood cholesterol levels and to control blood sugar levels by slowing down the absorption of sugar. *Insoluble fibre* (in wholegrain cereals, pulses, fruit and vegetables) increases stool bulk and speeds the passage of waste material through the body. In this way it helps to prevent constipation, haemorrhoids and diverticular disease, and may protect against bowel cancer.

Our current intake of fibre is around 12 g a day. Healthy eating guidelines suggest that we need to increase this amount to 18 g a day.

Free radicals These highly reactive molecules can cause damage to cell walls and DNA (the genetic material found within cells). They are believed to be involved in the development of heart disease, some cancers and premature ageing. Free radicals are produced naturally by the body in the course of everyday life, but certain factors, such as cigarette smoke, pollution and over-exposure to sunlight, can accelerate their production.

Gluten A protein found in wheat and, to a lesser degree, in rye, barley and oats, but not in corn (maize) or rice. People with *coeliac disease* have a sensitivity to gluten and need to eliminate all gluten-containing foods, such as bread, pasta, cakes and biscuits, from their diet.

Glycaemic Index (GI) This is used to measure the rate at which carbohydrate foods are digested and converted into sugar (glucose) to raise blood sugar levels and provide energy. Foods with a high GI are quickly broken down and offer an immediate energy fix, while those with a lower GI are absorbed more slowly, making you feel full for longer and helping to keep blood sugar levels constant. High-GI foods include table sugar, honey, mashed potatoes and watermelon. Low-GI foods include pulses, wholewheat cereals, apples, cherries, dried apricots, pasta and oats.

Glycogen This is one of the 2 forms in which energy from carbohydrates is made available for use by the body (the other is *glucose*). Whereas glucose is converted quickly from carbohydrates and made available in the blood for a fast energy fix, glycogen is stored in the liver and muscles to fuel longer-term energy needs. When the body has used up its immediate supply of glucose, the stored glycogen is broken down into glucose to continue supplying energy.

Minerals These inorganic substances perform a wide range of vital functions in the body. The *macrominerals* – calcium, chloride, magnesium, potassium, phosphorus and sodium – are needed in relatively large quantities, whereas much smaller amounts are required of the remainder, called *microminerals*. Some microminerals (selenium, magnesium and iodine, for example) are needed in such tiny amounts that they are known as *'trace elements'*.

There are important differences in the body's ability to absorb minerals from different foods, and this can be affected by the presence of other substances. For example, oxalic acid, present in spinach, interferes with the absorption of much of the iron and calcium spinach contains.

• *Calcium* is essential for the development of strong bones and teeth. It also plays an important role in blood clotting. Good sources include dairy products, canned fish (eaten with their bones) and dark green, leafy vegetables.
• *Chloride* helps to maintain the body's fluid balance. The main source in the diet is table salt.
• *Chromium* is important in the regulation of blood sugar levels, as well as levels of fat and cholesterol in the blood. Good dietary sources include red meat, liver, eggs, seafood, cheese and wholegrain cereals.

• *Copper*, component of many enzymes, is needed for bone growth and the formation of connective tissue. It helps the body to absorb iron from food. Good sources include offal, shellfish, mushrooms, cocoa, nuts and seeds.
• *Iodine* is an important component of the thyroid hormones, which govern the rate and efficiency at which food is converted into energy. Good sources include seafood, seaweed and vegetables (depending on the iodine content of the soil in which they are grown).
• *Iron* is an essential component of haemoglobin, the pigment in red blood cells that carries oxygen around the body. Good sources are offal, red meat, dried apricots and prunes, and iron-fortified breakfast cereals.
• *Magnesium* is important for healthy bones, the release of energy from food, and nerve and muscle function. Good sources include wholegrain cereals, peas and other green vegetables, pulses, dried fruit and nuts.
• *Manganese* is a vital component of several enzymes that are involved in energy production and many other functions. Good dietary sources include nuts, cereals, brown rice, pulses and wholemeal bread.
• *Molybdenum* is an essential component of several enzymes, including those involved in the production of DNA. Good sources are offal, yeast, pulses, wholegrain cereals and green leafy vegetables.
• *Phosphorus* is important for healthy bones and teeth and for the release of energy from foods. It is found in most foods. Particularly good sources include dairy products, red meat, poultry, fish and eggs.
• *Potassium*, along with sodium, is important in maintaining fluid balance and regulating blood pressure, and is essential for the transmission of nerve impulses. Good sources include fruit, especially bananas and citrus fruits, nuts, seeds, potatoes and pulses.
• *Selenium* is a powerful antioxidant that protects cells against damage by free radicals. Good dietary sources are meat, fish, dairy foods, brazil nuts, avocados and lentils.
• *Sodium* works with potassium to regulate fluid balance, and is essential for nerve and muscle function. Only a little sodium is needed – we tend to get too much in our diet. The main source in the diet is table salt, as well as salty processed foods and ready-prepared foods.
• *Sulphur* is a component of 2 essential amino acids. Protein foods are the main source.
• *Zinc* is vital for normal growth, as well as reproduction and immunity. Good dietary sources include oysters, red meat, peanuts and sunflower seeds.

Phytochemicals These biologically active compounds, found in most plant foods, are believed to be beneficial in disease prevention. There are literally thousands of different phytochemicals, amongst which are the following:

• *Allicin*, a phytochemical found in garlic, onions, leeks, chives and shallots, is believed to help lower high blood cholesterol levels and stimulate the immune system.
• *Bioflavonoids*, of which there are at least 6000, are found mainly in fruit and sweet-tasting vegetables. Different bioflavonoids have different roles – some are antioxidants, while others act as anti-disease agents. A sub-group of these phytochemicals, called *flavonols*, includes the antioxidant *quercetin*, which is believed to reduce the risk of heart disease and help to protect against cataracts. Quercetin is found in tea, red wine, grapes and broad beans.
• *Carotenoids*, the best known of which are *beta-carotene* and *lycopene*, are powerful antioxidants thought to help protect us against certain types of cancer. Highly coloured fruits and vegetables, such as blackcurrants, mangoes, tomatoes, carrots, sweet potatoes, pumpkin and dark green, leafy vegetables, are excellent sources of carotenoids.
• *Coumarins* are believed to help protect against cancer by inhibiting the formation of tumours. Oranges are a rich source.
• *Glucosinolates*, found mainly in cruciferous vegetables, particularly broccoli, Brussels sprouts, cabbage, kale and cauliflower, are believed to have strong anti-cancer effects. *Sulphoraphane* is one of the powerful cancer-fighting substances produced by glucosinolates.
• *Phytoestrogens* have a chemical structure similar to the female hormone oestrogen, and they are believed to help protect against hormone-related cancers such as breast and prostate cancer. One of the types of these phytochemicals, called *isoflavones*, may also help to relieve symptoms associated with the menopause. Soya beans and chickpeas are a particularly rich source of isoflavones.

Protein This nutrient, necessary for growth and development, for maintenance and repair of cells, and for the production of enzymes, antibodies and hormones, is essential to keep the body working efficiently. Protein is made up of *amino acids*, which are compounds containing the 4 elements that are necessary for life: carbon, hydrogen, oxygen and nitrogen. We need all of the 20 amino acids commonly found in plant and animal proteins. The human body can make 12 of these, but the remaining 8 – called *essential amino acids* – must be obtained from the food we eat.

Protein comes in a wide variety of foods. Meat, fish, dairy products, eggs and soya beans contain all of the essential amino acids, and are therefore called first-class protein foods. Pulses, nuts, seeds and cereals are also good sources of protein, but do not contain the full range of essential amino acids. In practical terms, this really doesn't matter – as long as you include a variety of different protein foods in your diet, your body will get all the amino acids it needs. It is important, though, to eat protein foods every day because the essential amino acids cannot be stored in the body for later use.

The RNI of protein for women aged 19–49 years is 45 g per day and for men of the same age 55 g. In the UK most people eat more protein than they need, although this isn't normally a problem.

Reference Nutrient Intake (RNI) This denotes the average daily amount of vitamins and minerals thought to be sufficient to meet the nutritional needs of almost all individuals within the population. The figures, published by the Department of Health, vary depending on age, sex and specific nutritional needs such as pregnancy. RNIs are equivalent to what used to be called Recommended Daily Amounts or Allowances (RDA).

RNIs for adults (19–49 years)

Vitamin A	600-700 mcg
Vitamin B_1	0.8 mg for women, 1 mg for men
Vitamin B_2	1.1 mg for women, 1.3 mg for men
Niacin	13 mg for women, 17 mg for men
Vitamin B_6	1.2 mg for women, 1.4 mg for men
Vitamin B_{12}	1.5 mg
Folate	200 mcg (400 mcg for first trimester of pregnancy)
Vitamin C	40 mg
Vitamin E	no recommendation in the UK; the EC RDA is 10 mg, which has been used in all recipe analyses in this book
Calcium	700 mg
Chloride	2500 mg
Copper	1.2 mg
Iodine	140 mcg
Iron	14.8 mg for women, 8.7 mg for men
Magnesium	270-300 mg
Phosphorus	550 mg
Potassium	3500 mg
Selenium	60 mcg for women, 75 mcg for men
Sodium	1600 mg
Zinc	7 mg for women, 9.5 mg for men

Vitamins These are organic compounds that are essential for good health. Although they are required in only small amounts, each one has specific vital functions to perform. Most vitamins cannot be made by the human body, and therefore must be obtained from the diet. The body is capable of storing some vitamins (A, D, E, K and B_{12}), but the rest need to be provided by the diet on a regular basis. A well-balanced diet, containing a wide variety of different foods, is the best way to ensure that you get all the vitamins you need.

Vitamins can be divided into 2 groups: *water-soluble* (B complex and C) and *fat-soluble* (A, D, E and K). Water-soluble vitamins are easily destroyed during processing, storage, and the preparation and cooking of food. The fat-soluble vitamins are less vulnerable to losses during cooking and processing.

• *Vitamin A* (retinol) is essential for healthy vision, eyes, skin and growth. Good sources include dairy products, offal (especially liver), eggs and oily fish. Vitamin A can also be obtained from *beta-carotene*, the pigment found in highly coloured fruit and vegetables. In addition to acting as a source of vitamin A, beta-carotene has an important role to play as an antioxidant in its own right.

• *The B Complex vitamins* have very similar roles to play in nutrition, and many of them occur together in the same foods.
Vitamin B_1 (thiamin) is essential in the release of energy from carbohydrates. Good sources include milk, offal, meat (especially pork), wholegrain and fortified breakfast cereals, nuts and pulses, yeast extract and wheat germ. White flour and bread are fortified with B_1 in the UK.
Vitamin B_2 (riboflavin) is vital for growth, healthy skin and eyes, and the release of energy from food. Good sources include milk, meat, offal, eggs, cheese, fortified breakfast cereals, yeast extract and green leafy vegetables.
Niacin (nicotinic acid), sometimes called vitamin B_3, plays an important role in the release of energy within the cells. Unlike the other B vitamins it can be made by the body from the essential amino acid tryptophan. Good sources include meat, offal, fish, fortified breakfast cereals and pulses. White flour and bread are fortified with niacin in the UK.
Pantothenic acid, sometimes called vitamin B_5, is involved in a number of metabolic reactions, including energy production. This vitamin is present in most foods; notable exceptions are fat, oil and sugar. Good sources include liver, kidneys, yeast, egg yolks, fish roe, wheat germ, nuts, pulses and fresh vegetables.
Vitamin B_6 (pyridoxine) helps the body to utilise protein and contributes to the formation of haemoglobin for red blood cells. B_6 is found in a wide range of foods including meat, liver, fish, eggs, wholegrain cereals, some vegetables, pulses, brown rice, nuts and yeast extract.
Vitamin B_{12} (cyanocobalamin) is vital for growth, the formation of red blood cells and maintenance of a healthy nervous system. B_{12} is unique in that it is principally found in foods of animal origin. Vegetarians who eat dairy products will get enough, but vegans need to ensure they include food fortified with B_{12} in their diet. Good sources of B_{12} include liver, kidneys, oily fish, meat, cheese, eggs and milk.
Folate (folic acid) is involved in the manufacture of amino acids and in the production of red blood cells. Recent research suggests that folate may also help to protect against heart disease. Good sources of folate are

green leafy vegetables, liver, pulses, eggs, wholegrain cereal products and fortified breakfast cereals, brewers' yeast, wheatgerm, nuts and fruit, especially grapefruit and oranges.
Biotin is needed for various metabolic reactions and the release of energy from foods. Good sources include liver, oily fish, brewers' yeast, kidneys, egg yolks and brown rice.
• *Vitamin C* (ascorbic acid) is essential for growth and vital for the formation of collagen (a protein needed for healthy bones, teeth, gums, blood capillaries and all connective tissue). It plays an important role in the healing of wounds and fractures, and acts as a powerful antioxidant. Vitamin C is found mainly in fruit and vegetables.
• *Vitamin D* (cholecalciferol) is essential for growth and the absorption of calcium, and thus for the formation of healthy bones. It is also involved in maintaining a healthy nervous system. The amount of vitamin D occurring naturally in foods is small, and it is found in very few foods – good sources are oily fish (and fish liver oil supplements), eggs and liver, as well as breakfast cereals, margarine and full-fat milk that are fortified with vitamin D. Most vitamin D, however, does not come from the diet but is made by the body when the skin is exposed to sunlight.
• *Vitamin E* is not one vitamin, but a number of related compounds called tocopherols that function as antioxidants. Good sources of vitamin E are vegetable oils, polyunsaturated margarines, wheatgerm, sunflower seeds, nuts, oily fish, eggs, wholegrain cereals, avocados and spinach.
• *Vitamin K* is essential for the production of several proteins, including prothombin which is involved in the clotting of blood. It has been found to exist in 3 forms, one of which is obtained from food while the other 2 are made by the bacteria in the intestine. Vitamin K_1, which is the form found in food, is present in broccoli, cabbage, spinach, milk, margarine, vegetable oils, particularly soya oil, cereals, liver, alfalfa and kelp.

Nutritional analyses

The nutritional analysis of each recipe has been carried out using data from *The Composition of Foods* with additional data from food manufacturers where appropriate. Because the level and availability of different nutrients can vary, depending on factors like growing conditions and breed of animal, the figures are intended as an approximate guide only.

The analyses include vitamins A, B_1, B_2, B_6, B_{12}, niacin, folate, C, D and E, and the minerals calcium, copper, iron, potassium, selenium and zinc. Other vitamins and minerals are not included as deficiencies are rare. Optional ingredients and optional serving suggestions have not been included in the calculations.

glossary

Index

Printing and binding: Tien Wah Press Limited, Singapore
Separations: Colour Systems Ltd, London
Paper: StoraEnso

index

Book code: 400-198-01
ISBN: 0 276 42887 0
Oracle Code: 250007855S